Residential Child Care

Residential Child Care

Collaborative Practice

Ian Milligan
and
Irene Stevens

SAGE Publications

London ● Thousand Oaks ● New Delhi

SAGE Publications Ltd
1 Oliver's Yard
55 City Road
London EC1Y 1SP

SAGE Publications Inc.
2455 Teller Road
Thousand Oaks, California 91320

SAGE Publications India Pvt Ltd
B-42, Panchsheel Enclave
Post Box 4109
New Delhi 110 017

British Library Cataloguing in Publication data

A catalogue record for this book is available from the
British Library

ISBN-10 1-4129-0850-7   ISBN-13 978-1-4129-0850-4
ISBN-10 1-4129-0851-5 (pbk)   ISBN-13 978-1-4129-0851-1 (pbk)

Library of Congress Control Number: 2001012345

Typeset by C&M Digitals (P) Ltd., Chennai, India
Printed on paper from sustainable resources
Printed and bound in Great Britain by Athenaeum Press, Gateshead

Contents

Acknowledgements

This book has been the outcome of a collaborative effort. In undertaking it we had certain factors in our favour from the outset: an agreed outcome, similar professional backgrounds, the same employer, and a shared outlook which values both residential work and social work. Many of our colleagues in the field do not always have these advantages when starting out on a piece of collaborative work. Nevertheless, we faced many challenges, not least the fact that this was the first book that either of us had written!

As we drafted our chapters we exchanged them, and had to get used to seeing our colleague's red pen put through our carefully crafted paragraphs! So we had to develop a greater level of trust in each other. Though there has been a lead writer for each chapter we have both contributed to them all. We are sure that we could not have produced a book such as this on our own, and while we cannot be the judges of the outcome, we commend a collaborative approach to you.

We were not working in a vacuum and we want to acknowledge the encouragement of our editor, Zoe Elliott, and the support of our colleagues in the Scottish Institute for Residential Child Care. Everybody in SIRCC is involved in the interfaces between education and practice, training and research, and depends on numerous collaborations, not least with each other, to get anything done. This book is respectfully dedicated to you all.

We also want to acknowledge the general support provided to researchers in the Glasgow School of Social Work through the regular meetings of the writers group facilitated by Rowena Murray and Andy Kendrick.

We wish to offer our thanks to Linda Gilgannon, Curriculum Leader (Health Care) at Motherwell College, Aileen Kennedy, lecturer in the Faculty of Education at the University of Strathclyde and Jane Prior, lecturer in the Faculty of Education and Social Work at the University of Dundee. They gave us very helpful comments on some of the professional issues and ethical codes in relation to health, teaching and social work.

The process of writing this book has been supported by our families. So Irene would like to thank Kirsty and Graeme, and also Peter and Ken, and Ian thanks Eildon for her support and tolerance.

Finally, Irene would like to thank Ian for starting this whole process and giving her the confidence to keep going. Ian would like to thank Irene for keeping him to deadlines, problem-solving and coming up with an endless stream of good ideas!

Introduction

Purpose and stance of the text

It is the contention of this book that the various forms of residential care for children have a valuable part to play in the range of services available to support children, young people and their families. In this introduction, we will be exploring the overarching themes of the book, and explain our rationale behind the use of the central terminology.

This book is intended primarily as a textbook for students on social work courses and we introduce the reader to the place that 'collaborative practice' has in the new curriculum for the honours degree in social work.

Before proceeding further it is important to note that the term 'residential child care' refers to many different types of 'home' or accommodation. The various forms of residential provision include secure care, therapeutic communities, special residential schools, as well as the more numerous children's homes, and respite (short break) services for children with disabilities. Thus we must be mindful of the dangers of over-generalisation, and only having in mind one type of facility when we use, or read, the term 'residential child care'. As we note in Chapter 1 it is important to recognise how residential services have continued to develop and diversify over the years.

Social work and residential child care

This book is concerned to examine collaborative practice as applied to residential child care settings. Thus the main focus throughout is on two sets of professionals, local authority-based child care social workers, and residential workers providing care for 'looked-after children'. First of all we will examine collaboration between these two key sets of professionals themselves and then we will go on to explore how both may collaborate with other professionals, parents and children.

However, before setting out on the examination of the various types of collaboration Chapter 1 provides a foundation by way of an introduction to contemporary residential care in the UK. Residential care for children has always been somewhat problematic for the social work profession, concerned as it is with trying to keep families together, and if that is not possible, then providing an alternative family through fostering or adoption. This has left residential care to be used as a last resort. Despite repeated appeals since the 1970s not to view it in this way, it appears that on many occasions social workers still regard an admission to residential care as some kind of failure; if not of them personally then perhaps of their agency. This book exhorts prospective child and family social workers to critically examine that perspective and to keep an open mind about the option of residential placement.

The quality of collaborative practice will have a major influence on the effectiveness of the care-plans for the children and young people in residential settings, and the transitions into and out of residential placement. When working well, collaboration strengthens the contribution of each participant and stops 'the buck' being passed. We believe that, as in other areas of social work, some degree of collaboration has always existed, but if we wish to significantly improve the quality of residential interventions, then better collaboration is a vital ingredient.

Foster and residential placements: complementing not competing

While policy since the Second World War has emphasised the preference for foster placement, especially for younger children, all major child care reports and reviews from Curtis itself (Home Office, 1946) to Short (1984) to Utting (1991, 1997) and Skinner (1992) have emphasised the continuing importance and role of residential placements. The problem of repeated foster placement breakdown has also been recognised by the same reports. According to Curtis:

> Children undergoing several changes of foster parents are often worse off than if they had never been boarded out at all. (Curtis, 1946, para. 461, quoted in Kahan, 1994: 24)

This message was repeated 50 years later in the Scottish review of safeguards for children living away from home:

> A good experience of group care is better than going to the wrong foster home, and infinitely preferable to going to a succession of foster homes. (Kent, 1997: 23)

When children themselves are consulted they often express preferences for residential over foster placement, as we shall demonstrate in the coming chapters. We acknowledge that foster placements will continue to provide the majority of out-of-home placements and that they are the placement of choice for most younger children but it is necessary to point out the dangers of an over-reliance on foster care for every child, and to take account of the views of the children themselves. The needs and wishes of young people often dictate the continuing need for, and value of, the residential option.

Residential child care and collaboration

We are supportive of the current government policy *ideal* of more 'joined-up-work', and its emphasis on evaluating the effectiveness of each profession from the perspective of the service user (Department for Education and Skills, 2003). However, there can be no doubt that turning such ideals into daily practice is far from straightforward. The policies are in place, and the local government and health structures are being reorganised, but effectiveness in practice will depend on the confidence, creativity and flexibility of practitioners. These can only flourish if there is support from managers. Practitioners setting out on new ways of working inside 'joined-up-departments' will depend on the leadership and example provided by their managers. This text aims to illuminate many aspects of collaboration and each chapter will explore some of the bridges and barriers to collaborative practice, the successful negotiation of which will determine the reality.

Having emphasised the necessity for all-round partnership some readers might be surprised that we also emphasise the *differences* between residential workers and social workers. Some would perhaps prefer that we see the residential setting as simply one among many places where social work happens, and would be happier if we simply referred to residential social workers. These issues are explored more fully in Chapter 5. We believe that there is a degree of overlap in the professional knowledge base and skill sets of residential workers and social workers. What is often referred to as the 'value base' of social work is largely common to both. The issues of values and ethics are explored further in Chapter 3. However, there are major differences in what residential and social workers routinely do and the skills that they commonly deploy. Given that these differences are not just about daily tasks but are reinforced by differences in pay, conditions, professional status and professional identity it is our contention that in order to promote collaboration it is necessary to recognise these differences and the consequences that flow from them. For example, it often happens that people start their social work/care careers as unqualified workers in a residential child care setting, then complete their qualifying training in social work and thereafter work in community rather than residential settings. There is rarely movement in the other direction from fieldwork to residential settings, especially after training.

We hope the book will be a resource for students of social work, and other professionals with an interest in looked-after children, and we especially hope that it will encourage residential practitioners, whether trained in social work or not, by highlighting the complex nature of the residential task, and the skills required to manage so many partnerships.

One of the implications of the drive to improve services from a user-centred perspective is that the organisational boundaries between professionals need to become more permeable. In this way it should be easier for children and families to access *all* the services they need, so that they do not need to undergo repeated assessments or 'get referred' to several different agencies. The delivery of social services, health and education in separate 'silos', with separate criteria and different access systems, has to be replaced with 'joined-up-working' and single assessment frameworks. However, the existing professions themselves are not being abolished! Residential child care workers, social workers, teachers and nurses will remain. Thus the question of how they can *integrate their services and expertise at the point of service delivery* becomes the key challenge for all concerned in the wide variety of residential settings where children may live for shorter or longer periods.

The stance of the authors of this volume is that greater inter-professional under-standing and collaboration is both necessary and desirable to improve outcomes for children in residential care, and can be achieved without any threat or loss either to the professions or the individual professionals involved. The book will focus on four sets of professionals: the residential practitioners themselves and the social workers who have joint responsibility for the children, the teachers, and the health profes-sionals (such as nurses, GPs, psychologists and psychiatrists) whose work can make such a significant difference to the lives of very vulnerable and disadvantaged children and young people.

Terminology

Throughout the book we will adopt consistent use of terminology while seeking to avoid modes of expression which are clumsy or stilted. There are two areas where there is a degree of difficulty in this seemingly straightforward task. We use the term 'children' to describe everyone under 18 years of age as this is consistent with the legal position and the United Nations Convention on the Rights of the Child (UNCRC). We also think that it is important to remind our readers, and ourselves, that even the older child is still developing and is therefore entitled to the support necessary to reach his or her potential. Furthermore, we are concerned about the contemporary tendency within a 'youth justice' framework to neglect the *needs* of children in favour of an emphasis on their *deeds*, in terms of what is now called 'anti-social behaviour'.

However, many teenagers, do not like to be referred to as 'children', and much pre-fer to be addressed as 'young people'. This viewpoint has been forcefully articulated by advocacy organisations representing children in care, and a formula has therefore emerged within social work that the term 'children' should normally be used to refer to those under 12, while the term 'young people' applies to those over 12. Thus when describing the range of those under 18 the phrase 'children and young people' is often used. We do employ this phrase at times; however, we felt that to use it on every occa-sion would be to risk producing excessively long sentences or awkward phraseology. We have therefore decided to make 'children' our main designation, with occasional use of 'children and young people' when the context seems to demand it.

A much more complex and controversial area is how to refer to residential workers. We have to acknowledge that while there is no universally agreed job title for those who work in residential child care units, the term 'residential worker' is the most commonly used in conversation and literature. Other designations include carer, residential child care officer, and sometimes residential social worker, to name but a few. With the registration of social workers has come the concept of 'protected title'. This means that only those people who have obtained a recognised social work qualification will be entitled to call themselves 'social workers', and this will rule out the use of 'residential social worker' for anyone who does not have a recognised social work award. However, it is the status associated with these designations which is the real heart of the issue, and one that will be revisited many times in this book.

As we address ourselves both to those who intend to work in residential settings and those who may work as children's social workers supporting children in care, we have decided to use as our standard designation the phrase 'residential workers and social workers' to reflect the reality of both different identities and qualifications profile. We also believe that, although they have much in common, residential work is a distinct profession in its own right. However, while we believe this, it is a simple fact that despite strong advocacy and many government reports and strategies over the years, residential child care has not yet established itself as a profession, with its own professional-level qualification.

As this book has a focus on practice around children in residential care the term 'practitioner' is also used. This is deployed sometimes just for variety and it is intended to refer to either a residential practitioner or a social work practitioner or both.

Collaborative practice in the social work curriculum

The curricula of all social work degree courses in the UK have their foundation in what is known as the Benchmark Statement for the degree (Quality Assurance Agency, 2000). The Benchmark Statement is a product of the Quality Assurance Agency (QAA) which sets and monitors academic standards for all university courses in the UK. In relation to the new social work honours degrees, the Benchmark Statement defines the knowledge, skills and understanding which social workers are expected to acquire during their undergraduate study. Due to the advent of devolution in the UK, and also reflecting the long tradition of separate social work legislation in Scotland and Northern Ireland the precise shape of social work courses varies across the UK. As well as the Benchmark Statement which governs the academic framework, course providers must make sure that their courses also meet the occupational standards drawn up by the professional bodies which include employer representation. These are expressed in the National Occupational Standards (NOS). In Scotland the Standards in Social Work Education for Scotland (SISWE) have been developed specifically to integrate the NOS and the Benchmark Statement. In this book we will mainly draw on the Benchmark Statement applying as it does to courses in all parts of the UK. The Benchmark Statement asks that social workers 'acquire, critically evaluate, apply and integrate knowledge and understanding from five core areas of study' (QAA, 2000: 12). We will now introduce the five core areas and discuss how a knowledge and understanding of collaborative practice is important in each of these areas.

Social work services and service users

This core area concerns itself with an understanding of the service and the users of that service. It highlights the importance of professional collaboration by pointing out that social workers must understand 'the relationship between agency policy, legal requirements and professional boundaries in shaping the nature of services provided in inter-disciplinary contexts and the issues associated with working across professional boundaries and within different disciplinary groups' (QAA, 2000: 13).

The service delivery context

This core area concerns itself with place and location of social work services from a policy and practice viewpoint. It highlights the importance of professional collaboration by ensuring that social workers understand 'the significance of inter-relationships with other social services, especially education, housing, health, income maintenance and justice' (QAA, 2000: 13).

Values and ethics

This core area looks at the values which underpin social work, examining their history and evolution. In the area of collaboration, social workers are expected to understand 'the conceptual links between codes defining ethical practice, the regulation of professional conduct, and the management of potential conflicts generated by the codes held by different professional groups' (QAA, 2000: 13).

Social work theory

This is the core area which addresses the body of theoretical knowledge required by social workers. In terms of collaboration, it asks that social workers consider 'social science theories explaining group and organisational behaviour, adaptation and change' (QAA, 2000: 13). Any type of collaborative effort requires adaptation and change, so this part of the core knowledge area is inherent in professional collaboration.

The nature of social work practice

This core area examines the characteristics of practice across a range of situations and settings. In terms of collaboration, it asks that social workers understand 'the factors and processes that facilitate effective inter-disciplinary, inter-professional and inter-agency collaboration and partnership' (QAA, 2000: 13).

Skills, practice and training

The section on skills within the Benchmark Statement also talks about collaboration. In particular, students will have to demonstrate a capacity to 'build and sustain purposeful relationships with people and organisations in community based and inter-professional contexts including group care' (QAA, 2000: 15). They are required to present information adapted to a wide range of audiences, some of whom may be other professional groups. These and other skills needed for professional collaboration are both implicit and explicit throughout the Benchmark Statement.

The training agenda within professional education programmes throughout the UK increasingly reflects a view that some element of *training* in collaborative practice is necessary to underpin the development of skills in collaboration. Documents such as *Learning for Collaborative Practice* from the Department of Health (2003) emphasise the need for approaches to learning which encourage collaboration, and writers such as Whittington and Bell (2001) make a plea for new ways of learning in social work and social care. They feel that inter-professional learning opportunities will be essential if students are to become confident in negotiating new ideas and perspectives with colleagues from other disciplines. Currently there are a variety of models being tried to see how best to incorporate a collaborative approach during training courses, and in some places social workers and health professionals are sharing some classes and modules together. Whatever the pedagogical approach to shared learning we hope that our book will be a useful resource for all those engaged in it.

Conclusion

From the perspectives of policy, training and practice, we can clearly see that collaborative practice is central to current conceptions of social work. This book has something to say about all these aspects of collaborative practice as they apply to children in residential care. We will look specifically at key aspects of collaboration between residential and social workers in the first instance, then with parents, with the children themselves as well as with other significant professional groups. If this collaborative perspective becomes embedded in the reflective processes of students, and indeed practitioners, at an early stage of their careers, then we are confident that the professional capacity of the sector will increase and the outcomes for children and young people in residential care will improve.

Perceptions and Realities in Residential Child Care

Introduction

Residential child care in the UK has changed markedly over the past 25 years or so. We have moved away from large institutions to small scale units and into an era of regulation. Additionally, residential child care's relationship with other services has changed. Perhaps one aspect that has remained is the critique to which residential child care has been subjected over the years. This book will seek to explore the importance of collaborative practice in residential child care and suggest some ways in which it could be improved. However, it is our contention that it is not only residential care which has to examine itself. We would argue that many of the services which work in collaboration with residential care to ensure best outcomes for children also need to look at their contribution.

This chapter explores why residential care has been subject to criticism and how it has adapted and developed in new ways. It is hoped that readers will understand why residential child care has been viewed in practice by many social workers as a place of last resort rather than a positive choice for children and families. By appreciating the historical perspective, we hope to encourage the reader to question some common assumptions in this area, with a view to broadening their perspective and thus aid the development of collaborative practice in residential care.

Learning Objectives:

- to recognise the diversity of residential child care services
- to explore the impact of placement policy on perceptions of residential care
- to understand the source of some of the tensions between field social workers and residential workers
- to appreciate the contemporary role of residential care.

What is residential care?

Before going into a more detailed examination of perceptions and realities in residential child care, it may be helpful to have a brief look at what is encompassed in that term. The Scottish Institute for Residential Child Care holds information on every residential unit in Scotland on the only database of its kind in the UK. This database categorises 14 different types of residential provision, ranging from 'mainstream' children's homes, to residential schools, to specialist disability services, to secure units. Some are long-term units and some offer a very short-term service. Others focus purely on 'short break' or respite provision. Some are highly therapeutic in orientation, others are more informal in their approach. It is important that any social worker recognises this diversity, as the practitioner needs to beware holding stereotypical images about a 'typical' residential child care worker or residential unit. In terms of collaborative practice, it falls to the social worker to develop an understanding of the specific type of provision in which a child has been placed. Fulcher has devised a framework of 12 variables which affect the function and shape of a residential service (Fulcher, 2001). He suggests that the social worker needs to assess the specific unit a child is in, or is being referred to, to understand the range of possible work and how well this will 'fit' the overall care-plan for the child.

Children can find their way into a residential unit through a number of circumstances and routes. One of the key background factors may have been abuse or neglect within the family home. However, children may also be in care because they present a risk to themselves because they are outwith the control of their parents or carers. They may refuse to go to school or they may be committing offences. Many children requiring out-of-home care are initially admitted to a foster placement, and residential care plays a significant role in both preparing some children for foster placement or admitting them after fostering breakdown, a very common experience.

In recent years there has been an increasing focus on forms of secure care for children under 16 who have committed serious offences and for those in need of security because of the risk their behaviour poses to themselves. Local authority secure units were originally developed as 'closed units' located on the campuses of the old Community Homes with Education (CHEs) in England, and 'List D' Residential Schools in Scotland. One trend that has worried many professionals is the fact that while there has been a marked decline in the number of 'open' residential school places there has been a steady increase in the number of 'secure places' (Smith & Milligan, 2005). While it has been policy to try to keep under-16s out of the jail system on the one hand there has been an increasingly punitive tone on the other about the need to deal with the 'persistent offender'. In England a completely new form of residential care has emerged with the setting up of privately-run 80-place Secure Training Centres. These are exclusively for children aged 12–15 who have received Detention and Training Orders under the 1998 Crime and Disorder Act.

Another major residential sector is concerned with services for children with disabilities. Many disabled children may be in need of a short break or respite service, and a few will need longer term care because their families are unable to look after them. A small number will also attend special residential schools during term time. The number of organisations offering short break services has grown since the closure of the long-stay hospitals. While the family is the right place for disabled children to be based, many families need support of various kinds to ensure that the child remains with them. Short break services themselves would also argue that they do not merely exist to give respite to carers, but that they provide a valuable service to disabled children by widening their opportunities. This form of 'rolling respite' constitutes a kind of shared care, which has become much more common since the inception of the NHS and Community Care Act 1990. Some disabled children may need longer term specialist support. One example of this is the growing number of residential resources for children affected by autism. Further examples could be given to illustrate the diversity of the client group and the range of residential services which has developed to serve their needs.

What do residential child care workers do?

It is beyond the scope of this book to provide a detailed account of all the tasks performed by residential child care workers employed in the huge diversity of provision that has just been mentioned. As with all social services, residential child care has not remained static. In both the disability and non-disability sectors, the size of units has changed from the relatively large-scale institutions and orphanages of the early to mid-twentieth century, gradually moving towards smaller, more community-based units of the present time. It has also diversified in terms of the range of services provided within or from a residential base. Some of these changes will be explored later in this chapter. While the diversity and sophistication of the residential task has developed steadily since the end of the Second World War (Berridge & Brodie, 1998) many people outwith the sector will not have much awareness of this process and may believe that the main, or indeed sole, task of the residential child care worker is the basic day-to-day care of the child in their unit. There is no doubt that good basic care does still constitute an important element of the residential task, and providing this is not in fact a simple or 'basic' task, in terms of the skill required to do it well. However, the residential role extends far beyond this, and moreover it takes place in an environment of awareness of the rights of children, and the expectation that staff will attend to and promote the rights of children in everyday practice.

Some of the tasks that residential child care workers carry out are determined by the particular type of provision. The pattern of the working 'day' for a residential child care worker in a short break service for disabled children will be different from the pattern for a worker in a residential school working with young people who have emotional/behavioural problems, for example. The key point to keep mind about residential child care is that it is a 24-hour service, with groups of staff working shifts to ensure that the best level of care is provided across the whole of the day and night.

In order to do this, the groups of workers need to have highly developed communication systems. Residential child care workers have to spend a significant amount of time on verbal communication in team meetings, and at daily 'change-overs' or 'hand-overs', and on writing and recording to maintain the flow of communication. Residential workers usually also have keyworker or co-keyworker responsibilities for one or more children. This means that they are the main person responsible for ensuring that the placement plan, which is derived from the overall care-plan, is implemented and monitored. As a consequence of this, the key worker has responsibilities for keeping the child's individual care file up to date, providing reports to whichever forum needs these (for example, care-plan reviews) and attending meetings to represent or support their key child. If the unit has therapeutic programmes which they implement (for example, cognitive-behavioural programmes) residential child care workers have to be trained and supported in their implementation. However, despite the increase in specific tasks associated with the development of keyworking, care-planning and structured programmes the most pervasive part of the residential child care worker's task is to attend to and take part in the daily life of the unit. This has been characterised by Maier (1981) as the 'core of care', which is marked by the 'rhythms and rituals' of the unit. Smith, writing on professional identity in residential child care, contends that:

> With its requirements to work in the moment, yet to connect the immediate to the overall experience of children and youth, is perhaps the defining characteristic of residential child care. (2003: 242)

It would probably be safe to say that there is no typical unit or typical day in residential child care. The residential child care worker, like the field social worker, has a range of intense and highly complex tasks to perform which are necessary to the well-being of the child or young person with whom they work. Adrian Ward has identified 'six distinctives' of group care work – aspects of practice which characterise residential and day care work and in particular denote its differences from field-based social work (Ward, 1993). He describes these areas as: the coordinated use of time, the focus of work, the interdependent team, multiple relationships, public practice and the organisation of space (Ward, 1993: 4–7).

The nineteenth-century origins and legacy of residential child care

Modern residential child care has elements which are both historical and contemporary. Broadly speaking it is a *type* of care provision which has been part of the fabric of child care for a long time but the *form* of the care has changed greatly. Although there were some antecedent institutions in the seventeenth and eighteenth centuries, modern residential child care can trace its roots to a variety of homes and schools that were established in the middle and late nineteenth century. If we look at residential schools – currently a larger sector in Scotland than in England or Wales – as an example, we can see that many of these have their foundations in the Approved Schools, which themselves grew out of the Industrial and Reformatory Schools. The local authority secure units, which also have education on the premises, grew out of the old CHEs/List D residential schools as we have already noted. Much of the modern short break or respite provision for children with disabilities is provided by the major child care charities such as Barnardo's, NCH and Quarriers. These organisations were founded in Victorian times and moved out of large-scale residential provision in the late 1970s and early 1980s for reasons which are explored later in the chapter. Similarly the local authority children's unit of today has evolved from origins in the workhouses of the nineteenth century, through cottage homes, to the post-Second World War family group home, to the contemporary unit of six or fewer young people. There are other types of units which have their origins in progressive mental health approaches, the 'therapeutic communities', which continue to play a significant role in England and Wales, but are no longer present in Scotland.

Activity

Think about the meaning of the term 'institution' or 'institutional'. This term is often used by social workers and others in a negative fashion but is its meaning always clear? When William Quarrier set up his village in Bridge of Weir – which at one time housed over a 1000 children in 'cottage homes' of 48 children – he declared that he was providing an alternative to the institutional care of the workhouse.

1   What do you think he meant by saying that his village was not institutional?
2   Is a 6-bed children's home an institution? If yes, what makes it so?
3   Why does the term 'institutional' have such negative connotations and can, or should, this be challenged?

Commentary on Activity

Sociologists often use the word 'institution' to refer to social structures like 'the family'. Places like universities are sometimes described, without malice, as 'long-established institutions'. Yet there are some who condemn all forms of residential care, no matter how small scale, as 'institutional', while at the same time recognising that the modern family in Western society now takes on many shapes and forms with widespread re-marriage, the emergence of lesbian and gay families, and the growth of households headed by a lone parent.

Questioning residential care

All child care practitioners should beware the dangers of over-simplistic or 'dualistic' thinking which labels any form of group care as 'bad' and any form of community-based or family-based care as 'good'. (Jack, 1999) As Jack argues it is better to consider any type of welfare as produced by a combination of state, community and family resources combining in a variety of models throughout history. Similarly, we should note that residential child care is evolving. While it is clear that some of the basic care tasks remain as they have always been – to provide a safe place, food, nurture and discipline for children who cannot remain at home – the care practice and aims of a modern residential care service, or 'intervention', are radically different from previous eras. The routes into care, the duration of the residential experience, its location within social services and links to other types of intervention are significantly different from the past and new forms of residential care continue to develop.

Nevertheless, the attitude of many social workers and other professionals about the role of residential child care can be ambivalent. While there is a reluctant acceptance that residential care is needed for some of the most troubled and troublesome children and young people, this is sometimes accompanied by a kind of wishful thinking that it might somehow be possible for all residential care to be replaced by other forms of care. As Kahan observed, the use of residential child care:

> has waxed and waned and waxed again depending on the fluctuations of professional and political theories and fashions and changing pressures on national resources. (1994: 4)

This kind of trend is not only found in the UK. Gottesman in a review of the development of residential services across Europe noted that the accounts from 22 countries:

> testify to two almost parallel processes: on the one hand during the last quarter of a century residential care worldwide has changed in almost all respects, mostly for the better; on the other, seemingly independent of this progress and quite paradoxically, the reservations, antagonisms and even hostility to residential care have grown markedly during the past few years, causing it to pass through its deepest crisis since the end of World War II. (1991: viii)

Social workers' perceptions of residential care

It may be difficult for those with little or no direct experience of it to understand just how modern residential care works. For example, a student social worker may have an image or a concept of a children's home, based on outdated information. The realities of daily life in a small group home or unit, the different dynamic of privacy and intimacy, the range of tasks and the styles of relationship may be much more unknown, misunderstood and indeed hidden from easy understanding. Lack of knowledge, allied to a professional suspicion of anything 'institutional', constitutes a hindrance to collaborative practice in residential child care. Government reports from the early 1990s (Skinner, 1992; Utting, 1991) suggested that all social work students should undertake a group care placement as part of their training. This proposal was not popular with many social work academics and it was rejected by the body overseeing social work training (CCETSW, 1992). Some of the reasons were to do with the lack of appropriately trained supervisors for these placements but undoubtedly it also reflected a widely held view that social workers did not *need* to understand residential care in order to become social workers, or that it was possible to develop the skills and understanding necessary without actually having direct experience and training within the residential setting.

Activity

One of the differences in residential child care practice today is that a greater emphasis is placed on respecting the individuality, dignity and privacy of each child. This is demonstrated in numerous ways, such as seeking the permission of children before showing a visitor into a child's bedroom, and knocking before entering, to give small but significant examples.

1   In this context how could agencies promote public understanding of what life in a children's home is like? For example, there is a lot of 'reality TV' around – should we invite the cameras in, if children were in agreement?
2   Care practice has changed but have the *needs* of children changed in a hundred years? Discuss!

The development of the critique of residential care

During the Second World War, as Bob Holman (1995, 2001) has explained, concern for children separated from their parents became widespread following the experience of evacuation. Towards the end of the war residential care was subject to very strong criticism launched by Marjory Allen's famous letter to *The Times* in July 1944 (Holman, 2001: 35–6). She was critical of the large, poorly furnished 'orphanages' and the lack of stimulation and personal relationships available to the children, and demanded that the government take steps to improve their conditions. While Allen's campaign was going on, the inadequate state of child care was further highlighted by national publicity following a shocking case of child cruelty. A 12-year-old boy, Dennis O'Neill, was starved and beaten to death by his foster-parents. The government instituted an inquiry into the boy's death – the Monckton inquiry – and shortly thereafter appointed a committee under Myra Curtis to examine child care services generally. At this time services for children were provided by a plethora of agencies and overseen by several different government departments. The Curtis Committee report (Home Office, 1946) into the needs of children 'deprived of a normal home life' made a number of radical organisational changes and set the policy direction that has continued to the present day. The Children Act 1948, incorporated most of the Curtis report recommendations and children's services became amalgamated into a single local authority Children's Department, to be headed by a new professional called the Children's Officer. The Curtis Committee had emphasised the importance of the birth family and a preference for fostering if younger children did require out-of-home care. There was explicit reference to the continuing role of residential care, with much emphasis on the development of less 'institutional' homes and a preference for the small-scale family-group homes (explicitly modelled on family life) where a house-mother (and father) lived in, often with their own children. In fact the Curtis Committee were so concerned to see an improvement in the quality of residential care that they rushed out an interim report focused on the training of child care workers. In relation to Approved Schools the report 'apart from criticising a tendency to regimentation, had made positive statements about the approved schools, seeing them as humane and well organised' (Holman, 1996: 19).

Relatively little has been written about residential care in the two decades following the passing of the 1948 Act. However, most seem to agree that, despite the criticisms of Curtis and the opening of some new family-group homes, change happened relatively slowly during this time, although some local authorities were much more active than others (Holman, 1996). The 1960s witnessed huge social changes including the widespread criticism of institutions of all kinds. Such a critique was fuelled by commentators such as Laing (1965) and Wolfensberger (1972). Laing and the 'anti-psychiatry' movement and Wolfensberger with his emphasis on 'normalisation' offered radically different approaches to treatment. There was also a series of scandals concerning the quality of care in hospitals providing long-term care for adults with learning disabilities and the mentally ill (Butler & Drakeford, 2005). Another significant change related to the wider acceptance of sex outside marriage and a marked decline in any stigma associated with being born 'outside wedlock'. One consequence of this was a dramatic decline in the numbers of babies offered for adoption. The 1960s also saw the growth and development of social work and by the end of the decade new social work departments were emerging, based on a generic conception of the social work task. As a result of the changing social relations and mores, and the emergence of powerful social service departments, residential care services, which still provided accommodation for about half of all children in out-of-home care, found themselves operating in a much changed and largely hostile professional and organisational environment (Crimmens & Milligan, 2005).

The analysis of the effects of institutionalisation as identified by Goffman (1961) and others gained widespread currency especially within social work, and the appropriateness and effectiveness of residential care for children came under strong attack from at least two directions. There was concern about younger children who were found, in the famous words of the Rowe and Lambert (*Children Who Wait*, 1973), to be 'drifting in care'. Commissioned by the Association of British Adoption Agencies this study of under-12s in children's homes found that many children were spending long periods of time in care, with little being done to re-unite them with their parents, or to find them adoptive homes. There was also considerable questioning of the effectiveness of Approved Schools in changing the behaviour of young offenders. Following the 1968 Social Work (Scotland) Act and the 1969 Children and Young Person's Act (for England and Wales) the Approved Schools were re-named as Community Homes with Education (CHEs) in England and Wales and List D Residential Schools in Scotland, and merged into the general child care provision. There continued to be considerable disquiet about the regimes in some schools, and their effectiveness in reducing re-offending. Alternative methods based on ideas of minimum intervention, and community-based solutions such as *intermediate treatment* (IT) were seen as the way forward. IT referred to a variety of forms of day care, based on group-work programmes which were *intermediate* in the sense of being half-way between leaving the child at home and taking them into residential or foster care (Thorpe, Paley, Smith & Green, 1980).

Under the new Social Work Acts the power to receive children into care and to develop community-based alternatives fell to the new social service/work departments. Social work managers were concerned about rising numbers of children being admitted to residential care and the need, on both cost and ideology grounds, to extend fostering and reduce reliance on residential places. This led social work departments, and the major children's charities such as Barnardo's and NCH to close most of their residential provision and develop new forms of family support services. As well as the development of Intermediate Treatment, more resources were put in to keeping families together with the support of the newly developed teams of field social workers. The pattern of restructuring, from the mid-1970s to the mid-1980s, was varied: some local authorities opened up a few new residential units to replace and re-locate larger ones, while others embarked on extensive closure programmes. Building their own homes gave the local authorities much more control over the admission and, perhaps more crucially, *discharge* of children from care.

The character of residential care during the 1980s

From the late 1970s onwards many local authority statements and service reviews proclaimed their commitment to the notion that every child should have a family placement, preferably their own. This approach was given a theoretical underpinning in terms of 'permanency planning' (McKay, 1980). Building upon an interpretation of Bowlby's work on attachment, the permanency planning movement emerged in the United States and originally arose out of concern about children languishing in temporary *foster* placements, or succession of foster placements. It had the apparently laudable aim of guiding social work practice so that every child would have a family which would support them into adulthood, either their birth family or a substitute family. It was assumed that such permanency, and the security it was intended to provide, could not be provided in a residential unit. Within this sort of framework, residential care could only ever have a temporary role – providing accommodation for a child until a family could be found. Even when repeated attempts at a rehabilitation home had failed, and when no alternative foster parents could be found, the fiction of the 'temporary' placement was maintained when it was declared in care-plans that a young person was being 'prepared for independence'. Given the emphasis on family, and the suspicion of institutions, it appeared that residential care was becoming a last resort. As a consequence the residential sector declined rapidly during the 1980s in parallel with the expansion of fostering.

During the 1980s the residential sector itself responded enthusiastically to the anti-institutional agenda, and the homes that remained became smaller in size or sub-divided internally. Keyworkers were appointed to try to individualise the care offered to each child and care planning began to advance. The differentiation of residential care also moved on apace, as units began to adopt more specialist remits. Professional literature began to emerge on 'the social work task in residential care' (Walton & Elliott, 1980). The demand for professional-level training for residential workers was maintained, and significant numbers of staff were seconded onto the Certificate in Social Service (CSS) courses which had been developed in parallel to the Certificate of Qualification in Social Work (CQSW) to offer a professional-level training course specifically designed for residential and day care workers.

Activity

Case study examining the innovations of the 1980s: a typical local authority versus a radical approach

Strathclyde Regional Council, one of 12 social work authorities in Scotland from 1976 to 1995, was one of the largest local authorities in Europe and it had the resources to undertake major research and review projects of all their social work services. The local authority produced two landmark reports on child care policy and services which both reflected the leading edge of professional thinking and influenced the rest of Scotland in turn. In *Room to Grow* (1978) and *Home*

(Continued)

(Continued)

or *Away* (1983) the Council laid out the roles that residential units could have and how they should integrate with fostering, intermediate treatment, and other forms of family support. The Council reduced its numbers of residential places for children, redeveloped its children's homes into smaller units with more focused remits, and they also funded and ran a large number of innovative services with the help of Urban Aid funding (additional central government funding for deprived areas). These included the Short Stay Refuge for Adolescents which combined short-term residential care, groupwork and intensive family work, carried out by the residential child care staff who performed the role of groupworker, care worker and family/relationship mediator. *Home or Away* suggested that each residential unit would have a specific remit such as:

- working with children while attempts were made to rehabilitate them with their families
- preparing children for foster care
- preparing children and young people for leaving care or preparation for independence
- providing supervision and treatment.

It was also recognised that some children might actively prefer to be in residential care rather than foster care, and that some residential units might care for sibling groups who would otherwise be split up. However, during this period numbers of sibling groups were split up under pressure to place the younger ones in foster care. This seemed to reflect pronounced anti-residential thinking that it was better to split up a family into several different placements, rather than keep them together, if the only place you could achieve this was in a residential unit. During the 1980s many authorities in Scotland adopted policies stating that no child under 12 years old would be admitted to residential care. For Strathclyde, with a much more deprived population, and a weaker history of fostering, the target was that no child under 5 years old would be taken into group care. The case of Strathclyde is an example of a typical local authority.

Some other authorities took a more radical approach. In the 1980s, Warwickshire attempted to shut down all their residential provision. In fact the authority closed its few remaining units, while retaining four beds in a voluntary agency unit (Cliffe & Berridge, 1991). This authority were not seen as doing anything that was exceptional in terms of the principles of policy, but only in the degree to which it pursued the 'familial-ist' policy.

Read the case study and discuss the approaches of the two authorities. Which approach do you think you would have favoured at the time?

The extensive closure of residential units across the UK in the 1980s, and the envisioning of its complete extinction by radicals, gave out a clear message that residential care was the place of last resort, and those who maintained a 'belief' in the value of residential care were very much on the defensive. However, by the late 1980s some voices were questioning the dominant view, recognising that it was damaging to the residential provision that remained. In 1988, a review of all residential services was carried out by the Wagner Committee. The subsequent report made a significant statement by choosing as its title, *A Positive Choice*. Although the Wagner Committee covered residential provision for all user groups, it was mainly concerned with the role of residential care for older people and adults within the framework of the proposed community care legislation. For Scotland another significant report, solely concerned with child care, challenged the anti-residential view by referring to residential care as *Another Kind of Home* (Skinner, 1992). The Skinner Report explicitly challenged the view that residential care should be a last resort and proclaimed that it should be a 'positive choice'.

The changes that occurred throughout the 1970s and 1980s have been set out in some detail in order to alert readers to the way in which these were driven by the new and self-confident profession of social work, whose attitude towards residential care for children was particularly 'pessimistic' (Butler & Drakeford, 2005: 183–6). Understanding this background illuminates some of the barriers to collaboration that exist in contemporary practice.

Residential care in the 1990s: scandals and recovery

The Skinner (1992) and Utting (1991) reviews of residential child care were commissioned by the government following a number of major scandals concerning abusive practices in residential care which emerged in the 1980s. There were the reports into physical and sexual abuse perpetrated by Frank Beck, a unit manager in Leicestershire. Beck, who subsequently died in prison, was able to survive in post and to be promoted despite complaints against him. A different type of problem was laid bare by Levy and Kahan (1991) in their report into what became known as the Pindown scandal in Staffordshire. In this case another confident unit manager had managed to develop an unacceptable regime for controlling the behaviour of children and young people. While the regime claimed a psychological justification which was subsequently exposed as highly questionable, it was clearly a very physically abusive system and one which again went unchallenged for several years because external managers seemed unaware or uninterested in challenging someone who was looking after a number of difficult young people.

The emergence of these scandals contributed to the poor light in which residential care generally was held. However, paradoxically, in raising the profile of the sector, these scandals paved the way for increased attention and investment. Given that most authorities continued to use residential care, albeit on a much smaller scale, government action was demanded to improve standards. Talking about the Pindown report, Kahan, one of the authors, argued later that:

> Its publication created shock waves which greatly heightened awareness in central and local government in particular, and made a new beginning possible. (1994: 46)

So the 1990s saw a great deal of professional attention being paid to residential care and a certain amount of research commissioned (DoH, 1998). However, even with basic questions about safe caring addressed and attempts made to increase the numbers of trained staff throughout the 1990s, there continued to be major questions about the quality of care as study after study emerged showing very poor 'outcomes' of care, such as homelessness and unemployment, low levels of educational attainment and poor health status (House of Commons, 1998). It is important to note here that many children and young people have poor educational and health standards *prior* to admission to residential care. They have also often had many years of other forms of social work intervention. In spite of this, residential care still tends to be the focus of 'blame' when these poor outcomes are measured.

Activity

Consider and discuss the effects of widespread publicity about abuse in some residential child care units. What effects may this publicity have had on perceptions of residential care held by:

1   social workers?
2   residential workers?
3   other professionals?

During the 1990s there continued to be a gradual decline in the overall number of residential places. In England and Wales local authority homes continued to close but were being replaced by increasing numbers of independent units run as private enterprises. Many of these units were, and are, very small, and there has also been the emergence in the last decade of single person residential unit. These are residential in the sense that they are run by agencies with other residential provision and are usually for young people with severely demanding needs, such as high levels of aggression and self-harming that may be labelled as 'challenging behaviour'. Scotland too has also seen the emergence of a number of single-person, crisis services which aim to hold young people for a short period of time until some more suitable accommodation can be found.

Despite the endorsements about the value of residential care and its place within social work by Skinner and Utting, residential care has struggled to avoid being used in practice as a last resort. The preference for fostering, and the perceived high costs of a residential placement, mean that it continues to be most often used when a fostering placement has broken down, or when fostering is simply not available. There are occasions when residential care is also used as a kind of 'choice' or preference but even these situations have something of a residual character about them. For example, when children and young people are seen as particularly difficult to place they will often be placed in the local children's unit, if a place is available. Residential placement is also sometimes used when young people are articulate and confident enough to reject fostering during the care planning process and assert their preference for a group care placement.

In 1997 a New Labour government was elected and Britain entered a new era of greater funding for education and health. Although social work continued to be under a degree of public and political criticism, the new government was prepared to increase resources and the residential sector in England was boosted by the innovative *Quality Protects* initiative. This was a Department of Health project which funded research and policy development in specific areas such as the education of children in care, their health, the use of recreational activities and the promotion of participation and advocacy. *Quality Protects* set out to devise various 'indicators' to help local authority providers of residential and foster care to monitor performance and drive up standards. It is also from this period onwards that we see increasing demands from central government for much more collaboration and 'joined-up' working in terms of services for children.

In recent times, residential care does appear to be more securely located in terms of the policy agenda and has become the focus of a number of central government initiatives which have aimed to improve the quality of the sector. As well as providing respite services for children with disabilities the sector continues to play a significant role in the care of some of the most difficult and vulnerable children and young people. It has become clear that if such children are to be cared for safely and therapeutically, then they need carefully selected staff that operate to high standards of professionalism. Thus the ground under residential care has shifted gradually to a greater emphasis on the *quality* of residential care. Evidence of this new reality is found in the call made by Sir Bill Utting for new children's homes to be opened up in parts for England (Utting, 1997). He felt this was necessary in order to create choice of placement; a choice which he felt had been much diminished by the systematic closure of residential units over the previous 20 years. Tellingly he made this call in his report *People Like Us* (1997) which was commissioned by the government specifically to look into the safety of children in residential and foster care following the abuse scandals.

The consequences of current placement policy: placement instability

Ironically the application of the 'permanency' approach to children of all ages in residential care in the UK led to a rise in the numbers of children and young people experiencing multiple placement breakdowns and moves. This seemed to be accepted by most child care professionals as noted in the evidence to the Short Committee (1984) which reported that: 'Everyone working in foster care is conditioned to expect a high rate of breakdown and this becomes a self-fulfilling policy' (1984: 191). As far back as 1946 the Curtis Committee had explicitly recognised the danger of assuming that fostering placements were always beneficial and the problem of placement breakdown was recognised even then (Kahan, 1994: 24). Having said this, it appears that the problem was recognised but the pressure to develop and extend fostering overrode all other considerations, as David Berridge commented in the 1980s (Berridge & Cleaver, 1987).

In 1998 in a Report by the House of Commons Select Committee on Health, concern was expressed after it was discovered that some children had 20 or 30 moves in their time 'in care'; 'uncared for parcels to be passed from one social worker or foster carer to another' (*Community Care*, 6th August, 1998, p. 18). Since then as part of the government's 'Quality Protects' programme, local authorities in England have been given a specific objective to reduce the numbers of moves made by young people in care. This is stated in Sub-objective 1.2:

> to reduce the number of changes of placement for children looked after. The measurement of this target is as follows:
>
> to reduce the number of children looked after who have 3 or more placements in one year to 16%. (Department of Health/Quality Protects, 1999)

While it is true that some placement moves are valid, and indeed planned, we might wonder if this is a good enough target. It certainly behoves all social service professionals not to become blasé about the impact on repeated moves on the identity, sense of worth, and indeed mental health, of children who experience such instability in the name of 'care'.

Children's perceptions of residential care

This chapter set out to look at the perceptions of residential care. As such it would not be complete without including the views of children and young people about the relative merits of residential care versus other forms of care such as fostering. Given the lengthy history of young people's organisations such as the Who Cares? Trust and Who Cares? Scotland, and other organisations such as the Voice of the Child in Care there is a fair amount of evidence about young people's views over a long period. A review of the evidence suggests that young people often express a preference for residential over foster care. Strangely this support for the residential option seems not to have influenced policy despite that fact that authorities have been under an obligation to seek the views of young people about the decisions affecting their placement in care since the 1975 Children Act and with increasing emphasis ever since. It appears that when children's views are elicited then local service planners and policy-makers have not given them much weight.

One of the first reports of children's views emerged from the groundbreaking Who Cares? Conference facilitated by the National Children's Bureau and held in London in 1975. The work of this event was taken forward by a group of young people and supportive adults, and advocacy organisations for young people in care emerged from this event. The report of the conference was published with the title *Who Cares?* and contained the following:

> When our group first met they were unanimous in describing foster care as a 'bad science'. They said this was the general opinion of children living in residential homes, many of whom like themselves had experienced fostering and its breakdown on a number of occasions. (Page & Clark, 1977: 44)

During the 1980s as children's homes closed there were numerous campaigns by young residents against closure. In evidence to the Short Committee, the National Association of Young People In Care offered the following opinion:

> NAYPIC would like to add that in its view the move towards community-based care is good social work policy and should be continued and extended. This means a wide availability of care within the community – we do not see fostering as an inevitable progression of this, it should be seen as part of the overall picture. It should not be seen as an obvious alternative nor as succeeding residential care and being somehow more 'natural'. (Frost & Stein, 1989: 115)

Various reports and investigations of residential care over the years have recognised that not all children can cope well with a substitute family. It has been noticed that some young people find that it makes them feel quite disloyal towards their birth parents, and the sustained high rates of foster breakdown suggest that it is not a happy experience for many children and young people. Recent research by Save the Children (Barry, 2001) continues to show support for residential care over fostering from those with experience of both. The respondents saw residential care as providing 'a more secure, safer and longer-term environment and therefore consistency of care' (Barry, 2001: 30).

Conclusion

Residential care has existed in one form or another since the seventeenth century. One simple fact underpins the continued existence and necessity of residential care; the demand for places. This demand continues, in spite of the strong commitment to supporting families and the efforts of social workers to keep children at home, and the frequent campaigns to recruit more foster carers. Many young people experience a period in residential care; for some it is a short period while for others it may last for several years. Often these children report that this is a positive experience. However, there is no doubt that there are major variations in quality, and young people can also be very critical of aspects of their residential experience. (Wheal, 2000; Paterson et al., 2003) We have already identified the problem of placement instability as children move between placements. However, it is also recognised that while social workers are under pressure to return children home quickly, this pressure may result, in some cases, in further problems at home and consequent re-admissions to care. To address these problems and to make best use of residential care clearly requires adequate resources and a great deal of collaboration between social workers and residential workers, as well as with school staff and health workers. Such collaboration needs to be based on an understanding that a residential place-ment is not something that should be avoided at all costs. The positive possibilities that good quality residential care offer have been clearly identified in report after report and more importantly by numerous young people themselves. In the interests of positive collaboration, professionals working with children should recognise the influence of media images and placement policy on perceptions of residential care. The lives of the children in residential care are often fraught and the challenges they and their families face are complex. It is perhaps to state the obvious to say that there are no easy answers. Nevertheless, each professional needs to take responsibility for doing what they can to make the residential placement as positive as possible for each child.

Further Reading

Crimmens, D. & Milligan, I. (2005). (Eds.), *Facing forward: residential child care in the 21st century.* Lyme Regis: Russell House Publishing.
This is a recently published collection of diverse papers on residential practice and policy. The collection includes chapters on black children in residential care, communication with disabled children, football as a therapeutic activity and much more.

Crimmins, D. & Pitts, J. (Eds.) (2000). *Positive residential practice: learning the lessons of the 1990s.* Lyme Regis: Russell House Publishing.
This is a predecessor volume to the one above. This volume has a similar mix of policy and practice papers; including topics such as an analysis of the impact of Inquiry reports by Brian Corby and another important chapter on the opening up of a new residential unit by a local authority. Both these collections also include a critical review of developments in secure care in England.

Holman, B. (1996). *The corporate parent: Manchester children's department 1948–71*. London: NISW.
Bob is an inspiration to many for his long-standing commitment to live in the disadvantaged communities in which he has worked. This is a sympathetic, but not uncritical, account of how a large children's department evolved. It describes the changes in its residential units in the context of the wider changes in child care that were happening at the time. This is an important volume because little has been written about residential care in the era of the children's departments (1948–68).

What Do We Mean by Collaborative Practice?

Introduction

We hope that this chapter will set the scene for the main topic of this book, by examining what we mean when we speak about collaborative practice. It will introduce the reader to the range of terminology which is used in this area. It will look at some of the practitioners involved and begin to address the roles of children and parents in collaborative practice. It will explore some of the barriers to collaborative practice and serves as a baseline for the chapters which follow. In particular, the chapter addresses the part of the QAA Benchmark Statement (2000) which deals with social work services and service users, by beginning to explore some of the issues associated with working across professional boundaries.

Learning Objectives:

- to examine the language of collaboration
- to explore definitions and clarify these
- to look at professionalism and professional power
- to begin to identify some of the barriers to collaborative practice.

The language of collaboration

Collaboration is defined in the Cambridge Dictionary (2004) as 'when two or more people work together to create or achieve the same thing'. An analysis of the QAA Benchmark Statement (2000) throws up several terms which imply the need for collaboration, including *inter-disciplinary, inter-relationships, inter-professional* and *inter-agency.* These sets of terms imply that collaboration is more complex than the idea of two people working together. Collaboration in this context implies the involvement not only of individuals, but also of agencies, organisations and professional identities.

Whittington (2003), in a helpful exploration of the terminology, felt that there were two subsets which tended to be used in the literature. One subset of terms (for example, inter-agency, inter-organisational) is mostly concerned with organisations. The other subset (for example, multi-disciplinary, inter-professional) is concerned with the professions or disciplines involved. He further drew attention to the use of the prefixes *multi* and *inter*. He argued that the former suggested operation in parallel, while the latter suggested greater integration. However, he admitted that in practice, collaboration varies around these types.

In addition, collaboration can happen at various levels. Booth (1983) suggested three levels of collaboration:

1   Collaboration at practitioner level: this is the work carried out by different practitioners aimed at meeting the needs of the service user.
2   Collaboration at operational level: this work concerns the integration of service delivery, at the level of the practice manager or head of service.
3   Collaboration at strategic level: this looks at making policies, setting priorities or allocating resources.

Another useful definition of collaboration is given by Biggs (2003). Biggs asks us to consider collaboration as working together to achieve something which neither agency could achieve alone. In this book we have taken up the suggestion of Whittington (2003) who feels that some of the terminology overlooks the contribution of unqualified staff and service users within the collaborative enterprise. He asks us to: 'think more broadly of "collaborative practice", an idea that unifies many of the terms' (2003: 7).

This is particularly relevant as we consider the range of needs of the vulnerable children and young people who are found in residential units, whether for shorter or longer periods. If their needs for better health or education are to be addressed, or if they are going to be helped to return to their families, or find a place in a new one, then numerous adults are going to be involved in their lives. Collaborative practice is indicated!

Defining collaborative practice

When it comes to exploring what is meant by collaborative practice, there is a range of terminology in the literature which we can draw upon to help define the activities which make up this type of practice. This wide range of terms is used to describe situations where people or organisations work together to achieve a goal. Some of the more common terms used are *partnership, networking* and *collectives*. Alter (2000) is not alone in pointing out that there is no agreement within the literature about standard definitions of the various terms. Easen, Atkins and Dyson (2000), in their discussion on the inter-professional collaborative experiences of practitioners in the children and families field, allude to: 'the conceptual elusiveness of terms such as coordination and collaboration' (2000: 356).

Within practice the above terms are often used interchangeably with each other. Hallett and Birchall (1992) in their literature review on child protection also highlighted the problem with definition. Specifically, they noted that the use of terms such as collaboration, coordination and cooperation are often confused. Although they have similar underlying connotations, they can mean different things in practice. It may be helpful to explore some of the terminology before coming to a conclusion about what we mean by collaborative practice. Building on Whittington's suggestions, the following definitions are offered here for consideration:

- *Partnership*: a relationship involving two or more people, groups or organisations where the relationship itself is achieved, maintained and reviewed.
- *Inter-professional/Inter-disciplinary*: where groups of workers from different professions or disciplines work together.
- *Networking*: a process whereby a loose grouping of people come together for a common purpose and to create links with each other.
- *Inter-agency*: where two or more organisations or agencies work together to achieve a goal.
- *Collective*: a situation where every member of the group has equal power, authority and a common purpose. No member of the group has any particular role, in that functions can be carried out by anyone.
- *Inter-relationships*: relationships between professions, agencies or groups of workers in the same agency, and their clients.

Activity

Look at the following descriptions and decide which of the above terms is the best fit for the scenario which is described:

1 A child care social worker, a residential child care practitioner and a placement coordinator meet to discuss a placement for a young person with mental health problems.
2 A community psychiatric nurse, a child psychologist and a residential child care practitioner meet to discuss a strategy of work for a young person with mental health problems.
3 A residential child care practitioner attends a conference on mental health issues.

(Continued)

4   A young person with mental health issues attends a local self-help support group for users of mental health services.
5   A teacher and a residential child care practitioner meet to talk about how they will encourage a young person to engage with their school work, both in school and out of school.
6   Police and social work management get together to develop a protocol for dealing with young people who abscond from their residential unit.

Commentary on Activity

On the face of it, this should be a simple exercise. Indeed, some parts of the exercise are fairly straightforward. For example, most readers would probably have identified networking as being closest to activity number three on the list, and collective as closest to number four. However, many of the other activities could have come under a variety of headings. For example, both activities one and two are inter-professional/inter-disciplinary. Number five is inter-professional/inter-disciplinary but could also be a partnership. Number six is inter-agency, but could this also be termed as inter-professional? And aren't they all about inter-relationships? It could be argued that all of the above are examples of collaborative practice, and this activity is designed to show how complex the field of definition is, and how important it is to develop a clear sense of what is meant by collaborative practice in a given situation.

If we refer back to Booth's discussions on levels of collaboration, the examples in the activity above represent collaborative practice at the practitioner level. In reality, in terms of outcomes for young people, this is the most common and the most important type of collaborative practice. Indeed, the scope of this book is mainly concerned with collaborative practice at the level which directly involves the different professionals and practitioners who directly relate to the residential child care unit. Although some consideration will be given to the need for policies and procedures developed at a different level, these will be related back to how they support collaborative practice.

The need for collaborative practice

As outlined in the introduction to this book, recent professional definitions of social work emphasise the importance of competence in the area of collaborative practice.

But why is this so, and what is hoped will be the difference in promoting a more collaborative approach? If collaborative practice is to prove worthy of the recent emphasis that has been placed on it then it must have real outcomes for the lives of children. Compton and Galaway (1999) point out that social workers spend as much as 30% of their time in dealing with other professions, so the need to understand and to enhance collaborative practice with other professionals is clear. Governmental agendas, perhaps more than professional agendas, have had an important part to play in determining the demand for collaboration and this was explored in some depth in the first chapter. A brief review of some of the governmental priorities regarding children will be made at this point, in order to demonstrate the need for collaboration. In England and Wales, the report by the Department for Education and Skills entitled *Every Child Matters* (2003) and its subsequent legislative impact has led to the establishment of inter-agency Children's Trusts. In Scotland, the report *For Scotland's Children*, (Scottish Executive, 2001), strongly emphasises the need for all practitioners involved with children to work together. The role of collaborative practice and the tragic consequences when this does not happen is perhaps best highlighted in the case of public inquiries into child abuse, both in the community and in residential care.

Activity

Case Study

In modern times, the issue of child abuse did not really grip the public imagination until the inquiry into the death of Maria Colwell. The inquiry report (1974) pointed to failures in communication between professions – health visitors, doctors, social workers, teachers and police officers – in reporting warning signs and acting soon enough to prevent the death of this child. Maria was a seven-year-old child, known to social services. She died as a result of being beaten and neglected by her stepfather and mother after having been in the care of the local authority. This inquiry was followed by a number of other inquiries over the subsequent years. Among the most highly publicised of these were the inquiries into the deaths of Jasmine Beckford (1985), Kimberly Carlile (1987), Tyra Henry (1987), and more recently Victoria Climbié (2003) in London and Caleb Ness (2003) in Edinburgh. Each of the inquiries into these deaths discovered a similar lack of communication and collaboration between professionals as had been reported in the case of Maria Colwell. Given that almost 30 years has lapsed between the death of Maria Colwell and the death of Caleb Ness, it is worrying to note the similarities between the cases. Hallett and Birchall (1992), in their review of the literature into failures to protect children, drew attention to the problematic nature of inter-professional and inter-agency cooperation. The various reports have made numerous recommendations regarding greater

(Continued)

collaboration. As a result, highly detailed procedures have evolved, and social workers especially operate within a highly constrained environment. Ferguson and O'Reilly (2001) in their study on child protection in Ireland commented that structures and procedures for inter-agency cooperation do not guarantee good practice. They point to the complexity of children's lives and the lives of their carers, and assert that a balanced professional assessment of the needs of the child can sometimes be lost, in the face of professional anxiety and a superficial adherence to procedures. The identification of collaborative practice as a key area of learning for social workers and others could help prevent future tragedies.

Question

There is a strong argument from the above that lack of collaboration was one of the factors leading to the failure to protect these children. However, taking account of Ferguson and O'Reilly's findings, how would you suggest that procedures for collaboration could lead to better outcomes for children?

Collaborative practice, power and the growth of professionalism

An examination of collaborative practice in the public services seems to indicate that practitioners have struggled with the best ways to provide help. Booth noted that 'the development of more effective collaboration … has been a prominent and consistent feature of national policy under successive governments' (1983: 10). While there can be no doubt about the strength of the government's desire for much greater collaboration this does not mean that such practice is easy to achieve or even very straightforward to translate into practice. As Kelly and Hill noted in a review of a project which did successfully integrate a voluntary sector service with a local authority children and families social work division 'differences in power, orientation and interests can lead to conflicts or rivalry' (1994: 1).

These are major issues that need to be recognised and tackled before effective collaborative practice is likely to take place. Simply having a generalised desire to work across professional boundaries or the existence of a 'mission statement', or even the creation of a single 'children's services director' (as required in terms of the Children Act 2004), are in themselves not sufficient to deal with issues arising from power differentials between professional groups, the influence of professional identity and how the interests of various professionals can be accommodated. It is our contention that these issues can be real *barriers* to collaboration but when recognised and addressed can become *bridges* which connect professionals involved with a particular child and their family, and produce more effective service delivery.

The New Labour government has been vigorously pursuing the promotion of 'joined-up' working since it came to office in 1997. If policy concerns similar to those of the 1980s are on the agenda at the present time, at least in the area of child protection, this suggests that the public services have not been very successful in their efforts at collaboration thus far. It will be argued in this book, at various points, that the growth of professionalism has not helped the development of collaborative practice at the practitioner level when it comes to residential care. Social work has struggled with its professional identity more than some of the other professional groups discussed in this book, due to the newness of its status in comparison to nursing or teaching, for example. This topic shall be revisited and explored at various points in subsequent chapters.

Recognising that there are differences in power and status, differences in professional outlook and differences in how the various professionals each understand the best interests of their clients may seem obvious and possibly embarrassing to raise and seek to discuss. However, especially in a residential care context such recognition is essential. The 'Cinderella' status of residential work within social work was first explored in Chapter 1 but it is sufficient to say at this point that the way in which other professionals view residential workers can create barriers to collaborative practice.

Residential practitioners need to recognise that there are professional differences between social workers and other groups whom they will sometimes meet with to discuss a particular child or young person. These groups could include teachers and a wide range of health care professionals such as nurses or psychologists who belong to longer established and higher status professions than social workers. When it is argued that differences in status and identity need to be recognised, this goes beyond simply asking practitioners to recognise well-established social realities. It is a plea to recognise the impact of these differences; for example, just because practitioners appear to be working together in a meeting or discussing a case over the phone, this in itself does not constitute collaborative practice, and certainly not effective collaborative practice.

Due to the professional understandings that exist within each group, social workers or residential workers cannot make the assumption that their fellow professionals will accept their definition of circumstances, even where the child or young person is 'in care' or the subject of a child protection enquiry. In most such interprofessional communications, social workers and residential workers have to recognise that they will need to deploy a range of interpersonal and communication skills if they are going to achieve the outcomes they hope for, whether these are procedural in terms of setting up a meeting or requesting a report, or practical in terms of obtaining a service of some kind for a specific service user. This is not to suggest that social workers and residential workers should only have to rely on 'charm' or a wheedling approach. There are a range of skills which workers must employ in a self-conscious way in collaborative practice and these will be explored at various points in the book. However, a good baseline is to recognise that inter-professional communication in relation to a vulnerable child, or a child who has been defined as 'troublesome' is not likely to be straightforward, and when it does go smoothly it may be regarded as a pleasant exception. There will be times when social service practitioners will face a lack of cooperation or understanding at all levels. This may require them to be assertive in carrying out their role. Occasionally they may need to be challenging and prepared to raise matters further up the line of command. However, social work practitioners require to keep in mind both their own professional identity and that of the practitioner with whom collaborative practice is happening (or not happening).

All agencies and organisations need be aware of these professional sensitivities, and develop agreements at all levels to support workers in their inter-professional task. Thus, for example, many areas now have joint health and social work protocols covering aspects of community care work, and similarly there is an increasing number of social work and education protocols relating to the education of looked-after children, and the management of children and young people considered to be at risk in terms of their school behaviour. These protocols are written documents outlining what actions various members of staff should take to deal with specific issues, and often proformas and specific procedural guidance have been developed. The impact of organisations and work groups will be further explored in Chapter 4.

Inter-professional negotiation: understanding agency contexts in collaborative practice

The development of departmental-level or inter-agency protocols are examples of collaboration that will have involved detailed negotiation that has been undertaken in order to facilitate better inter-professional working. But even in aspects of their work that are not covered by protocols, the importance of *negotiating* with fellow professionals has been recognised as an important pre-condition of effective collaborative practice by commentators such as Lewicki, Barry, Saunders and Minton (2003), who emphasise the importance of the interpersonal skills required to negotiate successfully. At its simplest *negotiation* can happen informally between a social worker or residential worker and a teacher or nurse and represents the next stage from simply *recognising* the significance of professional difference that has been noted above. Even where some tensions exist in a particular case, for example, if a social worker is speaking to a head teacher or guidance teacher about a young person who has just had an angry outburst and is threatened with exclusion from school, it should be possible for practitioners to engage in some degree of negotiation about what they are prepared to do.

Activity

Case study

An example of inter-professional collaboration in the above context could take place in relation to a child who is seen to be causing problems at school. By taking the child out of school immediately in the hope of avoiding an exclusion, while asking the school to stay their hand if they feel the child could benefit from a short time to calm down before hopefully being returned to the school, the social worker or residential worker may be looking for the education professional to recognise that a child in the care system is likely to be experiencing a level of emotional trauma in their life that needs to be taken into account by the education department as well as by the social services personnel. Undertaking such practitioner-level negotiation can be much easier when a general protocol exists to provide some further professional and management support for the discussion but it is important to recognise that education professionals do have a different outlook and their interests will necessarily be with the overall running of the school. In these kinds of circumstances it may be necessary for the social worker or residential worker to take on the role of advocate to assert the educational needs and rights of the children and young people with whom they work. However, this kind of intervention is much easier to implement if there has been a history of negotiation involving local professionals.

Question

At what stage should collaborative practice be considered for this child?

Commentary on Activity

The case study above has tried to outline collaborative practice at the fire-fighting or crisis response level. It should also be possible for social workers or residential workers to take the initiative and attempt to negotiate at the care planning stage with fellow professionals and consider how they will all respond to a variety of possible scenarios involving one or more of their service users. The complexities of working with professionals from the fields of health and education will be further examined in Chapter 6.

Professional interest

It has been recognised that the existence of different professional identities implies that practitioners will have to negotiate sensitively with others who may well speak a different professional language and have what appear in the circumstances to be competing priorities, which are difficult to reconcile. However, beyond these issues there lies another question which is sometimes disguised when all parties speak of acting in the child's best interests. The 'best interest' focus is enshrined in the United Nations Convention on the Rights of the Child (UNCRC), article three. This focus has led to a requirement laid explicitly on all professionals to act in the best interests of the child. For social workers and residential workers, this is explicit in the Children Act 1989 and the Children (Scotland) Act 1995, and the Children (Northern Ireland) Order 1995. However, how a child or young person's best interests are seen and interpreted may also vary by profession, and yet true collaborative practice can only proceed if there is agreement about goals. There are numerous illustrations which can be used to demonstrate the lack of shared goals. For example, if a social worker feels that the placement of a child in a residential unit is a sign of failure, then they may feel that a rapid return home is in the child's best interests. They may feel that their judgement is supported by research findings that seem to suggest that the longer a child remains in care, the more difficult it is to establish a return home. The residential worker may well have an understanding of the degree of difficulty that the family faces in living together and may therefore feel that a longer period of time in the residential unit is required. They may feel that their judgement is supported by the fact that a premature return to the family home can break down and children often have experience of repeated admissions to care. In this case there are two very different conceptualisations of 'best interest' in terms of potential outcomes for the child. Effective collaborative practice cannot necessarily guarantee or predict which may prove to be the 'right' decision in an individual case but some recognition of the different professional perspectives is required if joint work is to proceed harmoniously, whatever the care-plan decision is. Having an open mind and willingness to set aside differences will only be likely if there is recognition of the validity of the others' perspective, whilst retaining one's own. Turning such openness into respectful collaboration also requires a process in which the validity of the differing opinions can be openly discussed and no one position dismissed.

Collaborative practice and service user participation

The foregoing discussion has outlined the importance of professional partnership. However, this is not to suggest that this is the only arena of collaboration. In recent times, there has been a welcome shift of emphasis away from a perhaps paternalistic view of the 'helping' task to one which sees service users as active partners in the process. This is reflected in the change of terminology from 'client' to 'service user'. Parents, children and young people are being increasingly involved in their own care planning processes. Once again the right to participation is enshrined in the UNCRC, article twelve, and has been translated into the various Children Acts which require practitioners to seek the views of the child. However, while talking about the participation of young people has become standard practice, achieving it is a demanding task. Barton (2003) acknowledges the challenge of engaging with young people, and how easy it is for professionals to slip into a paternalistic or tokenistic mode. Involving parents and children in collaborative practice will be more fully explored in Chapters 7 and 8 to highlight the issues and practice possibilities.

Barriers to effective collaborative practice

As previously noted, Compton and Galaway (1999) asserted that social workers spend as much as 30% of their time in dealing with other professions, so the need to understand and to enhance collaborative practice with other professionals is clear. However, they also point out that there are a number of barriers to collaborative practice. The four main obstacles they describe are:

1   The myth that the only thing practitioners need to work together is the spirit of cooperation.
2   Helplessness in the face of the authority of another professional group, especially one which the practitioner feels is of higher status than their own.
3   Problems with defining the parameters of the profession.
4   The contrasting nature of the different professional groups.

Each of these barriers will be explored in turn:

1   **The myth that all that practitioners need is a spirit of cooperation**
    Given the nature of work in the public services, it could be expected that practitioners have highly developed relationship skills and a willingness to work with others. However, this myth is unhelpful because the assumption is that the ability to get on with others comes naturally and is not therefore a professional skill. Challis said that the notion of inter-professional and inter-agency collaboration 'rests on an implicit ideology of neutral, benevolent expertise in the service of consensual, self-evident values' (1988: 17). This myth or assumption can produce a barrier to collaboration because as it becomes clear that other professionals have a different value base and different training, the collaborative effort can stumble at the first hurdle. The extent of the differences in values, principles and ethics informing the work of different professional groups will be explored further in Chapter 3.

2   **A feeling of helplessness in the face of the authority of another profession**
    If you see yourself as being without power in a specific situation, then this
    can become a self-fulfilling prophecy (Smale, 1977). Berridge and Brodie
    (1998) in their follow-up study of 12 children's homes in England found
    that residential workers did not have as positive a view of themselves as they
    should have, given the complexity of work they face. In terms of the two
    types of authority identified by Compton and Galaway (1999), residential
    workers may lack both a feeling of authority of position (due to the poor
    image of residential care) and authority of competence (due to a lack of
    specific training and appreciation of the residential child care task). This
    can be exacerbated by the attitude of professionals to practitioners who they
    perceive to be non-professional. For example, Jordan (1997) showed that
    social workers and health care professionals had great difficulty in sharing
    what they perceived to be professional power with colleagues in support
    services such as day centres. These issues will be further explored in Chapter 5,
    when the key relationship between the residential worker and the social
    worker is examined.

3   **Problems with defining the parameters of the profession**   Conflict over
    who does what or whose job a particular area is can lead to major problems.
    It appears that practitioners in all fields require to define areas of overlap
    as well as areas of specialism. As Turner (1991) pointed out, professional
    identity is maintained by comparing and contrasting the qualities of your
    own group with those of the other group, creating an in-group and an out-
    group. This behaviour legislates against collaborative practice, and will be
    further explored in Chapter 4.

4   **The contrasting nature of different professions can lead to problems**
    Each profession sees the human condition from a different perspective, with
    associated different beliefs, assumptions and expectations. For example, a
    medical perspective is very different from a social perspective or an educa-
    tional perspective, yet they may all be dealing with the same person and
    aspects of the same issue. This can lead to a belief by a practitioner that
    their professional opinion is right and everyone else's is therefore wrong.
    Easen and his collaborators looked at the conceptualisations which profes-
    sional groups had of their roles and tasks, and how this might lead to prob-
    lems. They found that the ways in which professionals conceptualised their
    roles and tasks were essentially about a culture difference. They commented
    that 'the nature of professional expertise and of the training … were suffi-
    cient in themselves to have led the different professionals in the project to
    conceptualise their purposes differently' (Easen et al., 2000: 357).

In terms of parents and children as collaborative partners in the service, there can be
even more profound barriers to collaboration. Not only has the practitioner to move
away from a view of themselves as the exclusive holders of expertise and resources,
they also have to be aware of how the forces of oppression and discrimination can

work to undermine efforts to promote collaborative working with service users. Children are among the most powerless groups in our society and trying to redress power imbalances when carrying out a protective and statutory role can be difficult. It is very important for practitioners to analyse the power dynamics that exist between themselves and service users, in order to be self-aware about what this means for the relationship.

Throughout the book, particular barriers to collaborative practice will be highlighted and some suggestions on how to overcome those barriers will be explored. However, a good starting point might be a general understanding that all professional groups and practitioners are diverse but each has something valuable to offer. In the view of Bottery the development of an ecological view is needed by professionals. The ecological perspective is one that looks at the individual in relation to the environment or systems that they are part of. It demands that practitioners develop a view of themselves as part of a wider and interacting set of cultural, social and indeed political forces. As Bottery said, '[It] gives them the opportunity to see that they do not necessarily occupy the centre of any occupational universe, but are part of a much more complex ecology of occupations' (1998: 171).

Conclusion

A multitude of terms has been used to try and describe the process of working together, and sometimes this has led to a degree of confusion. The concept of *collaborative practice* may help to bring together the essence of the terminology. A collaborative practice approach is being advocated at governmental level and if it can be realised will have real benefits for children and young people. Developing collaborative practice clearly has implications for all practitioners and service users involved with residential child care. Professional identities and understandings can contribute to the construction of barriers to collaborative practice with other practitioners, but when these are recognised and acknowledged may enrich practice all round. Positive action from managers, agencies and organisations can have a profound effect upon the way in which services operate and the way in which practitioners are allowed to work. Power differentials must be acknowledged, both between professional groups and between professionals and service users, before productive collaborative practice can proceed. Collaborative practice calls for an understanding of each other's roles, and an acknowledgment that each practitioner or service user within the sphere is working to the same end, which is the 'best interests' of the child or young person.

Further Reading

Weinstein, J., Whittington, C. & Leiba, T. (Eds.) (2003). *Collaboration in social work practice*. London: Jessica Kingsley Publishers.
This edited collection explains how practitioners in social care, health and related sectors can work more effectively together in line with current developments in policy and practice. Definitions of collaborative work, policy and research are explored. The authors emphasise the importance of building genuine partnerships between professionals, and with service users and carers in planning and providing care, service development and research.

Understanding Ethics in Collaborative Practice

Introduction

Social work and social care are underpinned by a particular set of principles that should help define the tasks of social workers and residential workers and inform their methods of work. These principles, which include concepts such as the preservation of the service users' dignity, and the promotion of respect, individuality and equality, should permeate all of the activities that are undertaken in the name of social work and social care. However, while claiming to share these core values, it appears that social workers and residential workers approach the task of providing care for children from different standpoints. Furthermore, when social workers or residential workers have contact with practitioners from other disciplines, it may seem that the way in which those professionals define what care means in practice is alien to social work and social care. Commentators such as Tronto (1993) talk about how care is a different entity to different people, and the different perspectives taken on care by different professionals will be demonstrated in this chapter. If collaborative practice is to be improved, it is important that social workers and residential workers understand the tensions between their standpoints on care, as well as understanding the ethical basis of practice for other professional groups. The ethical basis of practice is often realised in the codes of conduct or practice for the various professions. At times, the existence of codes of conduct or practice may create points of tension and conflict between practitioners from different disciplines. This chapter will attempt to examine the ethical roots that may give rise to some of the conflicts between social workers and residential workers. It will also look at the codes underpinning regulation of professional conduct across the key professional groups of teaching and nursing. By exploring these areas, some of the most fundamental barriers to collaborative practice can be brought out into the open and understood.

Learning Objectives:

- to examine the nature of care in social work as distinct from residential child care
- to explore some of the philosophical ideas surrounding the concept of care
- to examine what care means for teaching and nursing
- to understand differences between the codes of practice for social work and the key professional groups of teaching and nursing.

The differing nature of care in field and residential work

Fulcher and Ainsworth (1985) in their work on group care with children describe how the tasks of residential workers are different from social workers. In residential child care, the tasks are focused upon care giving and the need to stay in the moment, working with the intensity of what is happening at that time. Residential child care also entails *being* with children. This means spending time with them in a range of activities of daily living on a 24-hour basis. Residential child care means having the ability as a worker to be in close proximity to the intense feeling which the child in the unit may be experiencing, and the associated behaviours engendered by these feelings. The ability to hold and work with strong feelings such as anger, pain and confusion, while accepting and understanding that many of the behaviours resulting from this and directed at the residential worker by the children are not personal, is an inherent part of the care task. Field social workers do not work in this way with children, and have a different set of assumptions underpinning their activity. Ward (1993) drew six distinctions between social work and residential care, and these were mostly around the fact that residential staff operate in the lifespace of the unit for 24 hours a day. On the other hand, the role of the social worker focuses on the management of structures to support the family, and the protection of children. There is little in the way of direct and prolonged contact with children. However, on the basis of this, would we say that social workers do not care? We would argue that social workers and residential workers both care about the children they work with. However, a deeper analysis reveals that the nature of care in each case is quite different.

Tronto (1993) discussed how care is conceptualised in Western society and argues that it is an *engendered* concept. Western thought has been dominated by the rational-scientific tradition since the time of the Enlightenment. In this tradition, reason is viewed as paramount, and the concept of rational thought became the criterion by which any type of work was judged. Tronto provides a feminist critique of how the practical activities of care have become devalued in Western society. Logic and reason became highly valued and seen as properties of the *public* realm of work and men. Care, feeling, and sentiment, being deemed outside the proper domain of reason, were relegated to the *private* realm of home and women. Tronto describes the *engendering* process, by which women came to be associated with the sentimental and *not* the rational, thereby denigrating the claim that care is a valued activity.

In the course of developing her ethic of care, Tronto outlines four levels of caring – *caring about, taking care of, care-giving,* and *care-receiving* (1993: 105–8). The position of social workers and residential workers can be analysed in terms of these levels. This analysis helps us to identify some of the tensions and conflicts between them. Tronto argues that the four levels of care coincide with specific positions of status within the structure of society. She suggests that, *caring about* and *taking care of* occupy the *public* domain of the more powerful. *Caring about* is, for Tronto, the *public* manifestation of the nominal willingness to care, and is the subject discussed when, for example, politicians talk about caring. *Taking care of* is likewise a *public* activity. It results from the policy-making of the more powerful groups and is translated into action by government agencies. For example, a police officer who returns a child to a residential unit after they have absconded could be said to be *taking care of* the child who has run away. *Caring about* and *taking care of* make up those aspects of care that are public and accountable in terms of the rational-scientific analysis.

On the other hand, *care-giving* and *care-receiving* are generally relegated to the *private* domain of the less powerful. The *private* activities of care have mainly been the work of women in Western society. Tronto would argue that the main tasks of *care-giving,* including those of tending to children, have been almost exclusively relegated to women. *Care-giving* represents the particularisation of the intention to care – it is care removed from the realm of the public and enacted in a context. One example of this would be the tasks of direct care (such as making a meal) performed by a residential worker in a children's unit. In this type of relationship, the *care-giver* is in direct interaction with the *care-receiver. Care-receiving* occupies a position different from the former three levels. The *care-receiver* is not viewed as the modern ideal of the independent individual. *Care-receiving* implies neediness and dependence. For example, a child in a residential unit would be the *care-receiver* in this analysis. So in conclusion, while *caring about* and *taking care of* represent the public, the universal, and the rational aspects of caring, *care-giving* and *care-receiving* represent the private, the particular and the emotional aspects. The first two areas have greater status than the last two areas, and these perceptions can have a real impact on collaborative practice.

Activity

Think about Tronto's four levels of care. Which level do *you* think the social worker occupies? Which level do *you* think the residential worker occupies? In relation to financial terms and conditions of work, which is the more valued in the public domain?

Commentary on Activity

It is argued here that social work primarily occupies the level which Tronto referred to as *taking care of,* while residential child care primarily occupies the level of *care-giving.* Berridge and Brodie in their study of children's homes in England highlighted the low regard in which residential child care is held in the field:

> Most significant is a negative perception of the service coupled with its low status. There has been a tendency for field workers and managers to see children's homes as a last resort and thus to use them for negative rather than for positive reasons. Hence residential care and carers have been undervalued and this has influenced their self esteem and morale. (1998: 180)

Research such as this alerts us to the fact that these barriers have a deeper foundation when analysed in terms of the engendered nature of care-giving, and provides an indication of why collaboration, even within social services might be more challenging than imagined.

The ontological basis of field and residential work

In addition to the different conceptions of care, it could be argued that residential child care and field social work are two different and complex entities, each with their own distinctive ontological basis. Milligan (1998) argues that it is difficult for residential child care to be professionalised when it is seen as part of social work and that it has a much closer affinity to the European profession of social pedagogy. In Europe, the social pedagogue undertakes a three-year degree to be able to practise in residential child care, and is viewed as a different *but equal* professional to the field social worker. The two different professions have different ontological bases. These distinctive standpoints are part and parcel of the different tasks of field social workers and residential child care workers. Anglin (1999) in his paper on the distinctions between social work and residential work comments: 'I knew in my blood and bones that the two represented very different orientations' (1999: 144). If this is the case, these differences can lead to real practice conflicts between residential child care workers and field social workers, and these will be more fully explored in Chapter 5. However, it may be helpful at this point to give a flavour of the differences, in order to contextualise the discussion on the different ontological bases of the two activities.

Payne (1996) suggested that there were three approaches to practice in field social work. The *reflexive–therapeutic* approach sees the social worker as working with the constantly evolving person, group, family or community, empowering them to take control of their lives. The s*ocialist–collectivist* approach sees social workers as having a more radical role in working alongside the most disadvantaged and oppressed groups in society, so that the power balance shifts in their favour. Although these two views represent part of the social worker's tasks, the predominant approach to practice is the *individualist–reformist* approach. This sees the social worker as a part of the larger provision of welfare service to people in society, responding to needs by improving the services within which it operates. It strives for an efficient and effective set of services to people. Given that this is the predominant approach to practice, we will now focus on this view, in terms of its philosophical underpinnings.

The individualist–reformist approach has its roots in the rule-based ethics of the philosopher Immanuel Kant. Some of the key concepts for Kant were the role of reason, the ability to make moral judgements based on general universal principles, and an impartial approach which views each person as an independent rational human being. He believed that no act was, within itself, either right or wrong. For Kant, it was the motive of the person performing the act which dictated its morality. In addition, he believed that people should be guided by a *Categorical Imperative*. Kant argued that we should:

> Act only on that maxim through which you can at the same time will that it should become a universal law. (1964: 88)

In other words, Kant believed that people should be able to develop rules of order, or duties which allowed this categorical imperative to be promoted. The categorical imperative has been expressed more colloquially as 'Do unto others what you would have done to yourself' and is an imperative because people must obey it; otherwise people would be betraying their own rationality, which is the foundation of Kantian rule-based ethics. When examining the tasks of social workers, it becomes clear that their actions are guided by rule-based ethics. Clark writing on social work ethics continually alludes to the rule-based approach in his examples of how social workers should approach dilemmas:

> Social work is legitimated by state authority. Social workers cannot give priority to their private judgement of client actions over key principles of law and accepted morality. (2000: 156)

In contrast to Kantian ethics, it is argued here that residential child care as currently practised is underpinned by, and is better understood in terms of, an ethic of care. Much of the debate in the 'ethics of care' grew from feminist critiques such as that of Gilligan (1982) who claimed that she heard a distinctive moral voice among the women who were the subjects of her research. She called this voice *the voice of care*. This voice emphasised the equal moral worth of all people, and said that informal and interpersonal relationships were a worthy area of debate in relation to morality. Care ethics give a foundation to the last two levels of care in Tronto's analysis. Care ethics reject impartiality, insist on the need to be sensitive to others, and emphasise the central place of concern and sentiment. Unlike Kantian ethics, which would insist that the same principles should hold for all people in the same situation with no exceptions, care ethics is averse to this and insists that judgements require sensitivity to the particular moral features of each situation. In addition, as Noddings (1996) indicated, care ethics would suggest that care is not happening unless the person who is cared-for actually experiences the feeling of being cared-for by a care giver. Noddings says that the experience of actually being cared for makes the care-receiver feel like a subject. On the other hand if a care-provider claims they care for someone but that person being cared for does not really feel that care, they may feel like an object rather than a person. She is critical of some of the agencies set up to care:

> The fact is that many of us have been reduced to cases by the very machinery that has been instituted to care for us. (1996: 27)

Care ethics is becoming a much more widely debated area for field social work as well as residential child care. Commentators such as Meagher and Parton (2004) argue that social workers should begin to re-engage with the ideas about care and use care ethics as a means to inform their work. Prior (forthcoming) discussed the place of virtue ethics in helping social workers to conceptualise their task. Virtue ethics are those which emphasise moral character, in contrast to the approach which emphasises duties or rules (deontology). A virtue is a disposition which is well entrenched in its possessor, something that is a deep and integral part of their being. A virtue is concerned with actions, emotions and emotional reactions, choices, values, perceptions, attitudes and interests. Virtues must be accompanied by *phronesis* or practical wisdom, and *eudaimonia* or happiness. In other words, a virtue must be practised in the conduct of living, and the practice of that virtue must be central to the person's sense of happiness or well-being. To possess a virtue is to be a certain sort of person with a certain complex mindset. Prior argues that care is a virtue which is highly relevant to social work. She suggests moving away from sole reliance on the rational-scientific approach and instead to pay attention to how practice has developed through traditions, history and 'small narratives'. By adopting such perspectives social work can begin to re-think the basis of practice:

> The concept of practice can be used to explain shared understanding. Through participating in a practice citizens come to achieve the goods (skills) internal to it and therefore through this pursuit, citizens can attain virtues inherent in practice. It is through communities of practice that virtues and goods come to be held in common since such communities develop shared meanings that unite them. In other words communities define the virtues of a practice and in so doing develop shared meanings. (Prior, 2005: 24)

These commentators argue for a redefinition of, and a re-engagement with care by social workers and it may be that this approach to ethics and practice will inform future debate. It may also be a key to bringing conceptualisations of residential child care and social work closer together, and thus developing a deeper shared basis for collaborative practice.

Activity

Imagine you are working with a 14-year-old young person who has been placed in a children's unit due to issues around self-harm. The young person has been cutting themselves, misusing drugs and is sexually promiscuous. As a social worker, what kind of contact do you think you would have with the young person? As a residential worker, what would your contact be like? What feelings do you have for the young person and how do they guide your work? Discuss the different types of priorities each of the workers would have. How do you decide how to prioritise the work that needs to be done?

The importance of ethics in professional identity

The concept of professionalism was discussed in Chapter 2, and is a fundamental idea when analysing collaborative practice. If the various professionals working with children cannot understand the importance of each other's professional identity, conflicts can arise. Professionalism as a concept arose in the wake of the rational-scientific tradition. The sociologist Weber, as discussed in Haralambos (2000) first illustrated the link between emerging organisations and the development of professions which protect their own interests. This includes the development and authorisation of a specific professional knowledge base, the setting of institutional controls and the promotion of specific material interests and group power relations. Over time, what were originally individual subjective actions become categorised and translated into professional rationalities. The profession is born.

In the UK, there has been a growing development of the professionalisation of public services. Social work is one of the newer professions that have developed in response to changes in society. In the 1960s, the establishment of social work departments in Scotland, and social services departments in England and Wales, gave the main impetus to social work as a unified profession. The Central Council for Education and Training in Social Work (CCETSW) was established in 1970 to regulate the education of social workers. This gave a further boost to professionalisation. However, even within professions that have been established for a longer period of time, such as nursing or teaching, there have been developments. Policy-makers and funding agencies demand that services demonstrate value for money. In England, for example, the Office of the Deputy Prime Minister oversees the Local Government Directorate (LGD). Within the LGD are teams which monitor the delivery of 'Best Value' for local government. In Scotland, 'Best Value' became a statutory duty following the Local Government in Scotland Act 2003. Public scrutiny, increased expectations, and the degree of knowledge demanded from the various professions identified have been rising rapidly. Practitioners within these areas are now often in a continuous situation of change and learning, partly due to the demands of continuing professional development, partly due to technological advances and partly due to the public policy climate.

Increased regulation and scrutiny, as outlined previously, have operated to raise external expectations about what the professional should be. However, the idea of professional identity is also important when looking at ethics. Identity is a psychological concept which looks at the congruence between an individual and a social reality. In terms of professional identity, the social reality we are discussing is the work role. Closely tied to this concept of professional identity in relation to the public services is the concept of vocation. Vocation is defined as: 'a type of work that you feel you are suited to doing and to which you should give all your time and energy' (Cambridge dictionary online). Teachers, nurses and social workers will often use the word vocation when describing their work. The idea of vocation goes beyond simply having a job. It is almost as if the job itself becomes a defining characteristic of the person, and that the activities associated with the job are a part of the individual's make up. Professionals such as nurses and teachers are deeply involved in their personal and professional development. Indeed, often it may not be possible to distinguish clearly between professionally orientated learning and personal development. For example, in the study by Brolinson, Price and Ditmyer (2001) on nurses' knowledge and perceptions of complementary medical practices, 79% of the nurses surveyed said that their professional preparation in the area of complementary and alternative medicine was 'fair' or 'poor'. More interestingly, 52% identified the general mass media and their own personal interest and research as their primary source of information on complementary medicine, many having used their own time and money to seek out the extra information.

We would argue here that the development of professional identity has three elements. One of these is the practice of work, which may contain some contradictory conditions. In a profession, the work is bounded by legal and ethical guidelines. The institutional features that develop to protect the profession can end up taking away the ability of the person to show initiative. One example of this would be the introduction of complementary therapies into mainstream medical care. Such therapies (and the therapists who employ them) can be seen by some as a threat to the profession and strong sanctions can be applied to members of the profession who use them. Yet many nurses would in reality uphold the benefits of some of the complementary therapies, as was illustrated above by Brolinson et al. (2001). The second element is the social interaction with other people (colleagues, clients and other professionals) and how this relates to professional identity. Strict boundaries and rituals can be drawn up to define relationships, and these boundaries and rituals could be a potential barrier to collaborative practice by the professional. The third element is the existence and development of the professional discourse, either academic or experiential. In relation to social work education, Karger (1983) questioned the value of having sets of 'scientifically' derived theories which are actually of little value to the practitioner and only serve to enhance the status of the profession. However, it has to be recognised that the development of a specialist body of knowledge is one of the characteristic features of a profession.

Nursing has been a long-standing public service activity. However, as Lempp (1995) indicates, although there is much to celebrate in the development of nursing, there are some nurses who have been in practice for many years and feel that the growing professionalisation and *academising* of their domain can be a threat to their perception of the core content of their work. They became nurses at a time where the core function was practical caring and human contact with patients. Their professional competence was grounded in practical experience. However, newer nurses who have undertaken a degree route into nursing may argue that knowledge and academic excellence is an important precursor of patient care. Therefore, professional identity will often take the character of a generational relation between old and new members of the profession, creating intra-professional points of conflict and debate.

Teaching practice has also undergone significant changes over the past 30 years. Methodologies have changed, content is much more prescribed and the whole profession and activity is subject to greater public scrutiny and accountability. Many teachers would define the core of their work as the teaching of subjects in a way that involves and engages the children and young people with whom they work. The professional identity of the teacher can be viewed as promoting the intellectual growth of children, and a teacher's traditional image in the past might have been viewed as that of a role model with an aura of caring authority. Many teachers traditionally worked beyond normal work hours and used experiences and issues that they came across in real life as potential material for their teaching. However, many teachers may now say that changes in working conditions challenge their professional identity. Teachers face new regulations about duties, the imposition of targets and changes to curriculum policy. There is also the expectation that teachers should manage all of the problems of their pupils while the number of pupils with specific individual needs is increasing due to the policy of social inclusion. All of this takes time and also takes away from what teachers would define as their core activity of teaching subjects in a caring and involved way.

The conflicted issues within the various professions can have an impact on how those professionals engage with social workers and residential workers. It is helpful for social workers and residential workers to recognise this when developing collaborative relationships. Teaching and nursing are complex activities, and collaborative practice requires that residential workers and social workers have an understanding of some of the issues discussed above which may permeate their way into the working relationships with these professional groups.

Exploring understandings of care held by professionals working with looked-after children

For the purposes of this book we have been focusing on nursing, teaching, social work and residential child care as the key professionals involved in residential child care. In terms of collaborative practice, all of these practitioners could be said to be in the business of care. It is therefore worth spending a little time looking at how care might be conceptualised by these different professionals, before the various professional codes of practice and the conceptual links between them are examined.

Earlier in this chapter, Tronto's four levels of care were discussed in relation to how society views and values care. However, in addition to this, there are the individual understandings which people may have about what *they* think constitutes care. According to Reich (1995), the history of care reveals that it is not a unified idea but is, rather, an interlinked family of concepts. The ways in which individuals view care can be grouped into four main sets of ideas. These are:

1   Care as troubles or grief.
2   Care as something that matters to the person who feels care.
3   Care as a duty to perform tasks for others.
4   Care as paying attention to someone's growth and development.

If different individuals hold different perceptions about what care means to them, it is easy to see how the four sets of ideas can create tensions between people. For example, care as the duty to perform tasks for others (dependence) can easily conflict with care as enabling growth (independence). When the roles of the different professional groups are examined, it can be seen that individuals within each of the professional groups may have different understandings of duty of care in their practice; that is, the idea of the duty of care underpinning their work can be fundamentally different from professional to professional. If the professionals discussed here are driven, even partially, by a sense of vocation, as discussed earlier in this chapter, it could be argued that the second notion of care applies to all of the groups being examined here. However, other professionals might have another notion of care as the main determinant of their practice. For example, a teacher could be informed in the main by the fourth notion of care. A nurse might be more informed by the third notion of care. We would argue here that social workers operate mostly from the fourth notion of care, while residential child care workers are equally informed by the third and fourth notion, due to the fact that they are in constant direct contact with the children and young people with whom they work, and that they are often called upon to perform direct care tasks. However, it is also important to recognise that not everybody in a particular group will have the same view or understanding of what their care task is.

Activity

Look at these examples of common or typical tasks undertaken by each of the following:

- a social worker carrying out an assessment for a disabled child in need of additional support to remain in their family and at their school
- a residential child care worker helping a teenager to change their bed and wash their laundry
- a nurse changing the dressings on a patient with a wound after an operation
- a teacher setting a homework task.

Discuss which of Reich's four notions of care appears to underpin the task you have identified. How might this notion of care affect their professional identity?

Commentary on Activity

A social worker in a children and families team writes an assessment for a disabled child in need of additional support to remain in their family and at their school. This will enable the child person to remain in their community for longer and reflects the fourth notion of care.

A residential worker helps a teenager to change their bed and wash their laundry. This teaches the young person independent living skills, while actually carrying out a practical task. Hence this reflects notions three and four.

A nurse changes the dressings on a patient with a wound after an operation. This is a practical task, which the patient could not carry out for themselves and is an example of the third notion of care.

A teacher sets a homework task, which encourages a young person to find out about their local community. This enhances the child's knowledge, develops their writing skills, and allows them to use problem-solving. All of this contributes to their growth and development in line with the fourth notion of care.

If an understanding of care differs from one person to another, it may be that some misunderstandings could arise from this. In terms of collaborative practice, having a framework for conceptualising the possible different understandings of care may assist practitioners across disciplines to overcome misunderstandings. In addition, all of Reich's notions of care are underpinned by the concept of *concern*. Everyone who says they care, in whatever way, shares the basic element of concern, be that concern for the one needing care, or concern about the circumstances surrounding the need for care. This is the part of the equation that demonstrates the existence of a common ground to work from. All groups of staff working with children share concern for them, and should therefore be able to find a common ground for collaborative practice based on this shared concern, even if they have divergent 'understandings' of care.

Ethics and morals, and their relationship to codes of practice

Ethics is defined as: 'the study of what morally is right and what is not' (Cambridge dictionary online). In essence the fundamental question of ethics addresses how a person chooses to live their life. Rudd (Reich, 1995) takes this further and says that ethics needs to be informed by a concerned individual's search for meaning. Here, the notion of concern is raised again. The concept of morals is also important. Morals are defined: 'as standards relating to good or bad behaviour, fairness, honesty etc. which each person believes' (Cambridge dictionary online). Concern is: 'the impetus for the resolute moral action of the self-reflecting individual who acts with a purpose' (Cambridge dictionary online).

The codes of practice for different sets of workers represent a supposedly objective statement about how professionals should approach their work. This is related to the ethical actions that they take and the moral purposes of those actions. In other words, codes of practice should reflect the ethics and morals of the profession. Hence, the codes of practice will be briefly examined to see what they tell us about the respective professions view of *care*.

The code of practice for social services personnel

Social work in England is regulated by the General Social Care Council. In Scotland it is regulated by the Scottish Social Services Council. The codes of practice for social workers and residential child care workers in England and Scotland were produced in 2002 and are the same for both countries (General Social Care Council, 2002). The codes of practice have six broad areas, which are further broken down into separate standards. The six broad areas are as follows:

1　Protect the rights and promote the interests of service users and carers.
2　Strive to establish and maintain the trust and confidence of service users and carers.

3 Promote the independence of service users while protecting them as far as possible from danger or harm.
4 Respect the rights of service users whilst seeking to ensure that their behaviour does not harm themselves or other people.
5 Uphold public trust and confidence in social services.
6 Be accountable for the quality of their work and take responsibility for maintaining and improving their knowledge and skills.

The sixth statement contains within it the obligation to work with others. In one of its standards it specifically states:

> You shall recognise and respect the roles and expertise of workers from other agencies and work in partnership with them. (Section Six; para. 6.7, 2002)

The concept of care contained within the code of practice is akin to Reich's idea of care as paying attention to someone's growth and development. The social worker would see that this is closely aligned to the types of task they perform. However, the residential child care worker is also informed by the Reich's notions of care as performing practical tasks for a person. So already we see potential for a source of tension between the social worker and the residential worker about where their priorities lie in terms of the actual work that they carry out. This is in spite of sharing the same codes of practice. When examining the standards, their rationale is to ensure that social services personnel provide help to those in need. The social work legislation across the UK places an overarching duty on local authorities to promote social welfare.

However, the way in which a social worker promotes social welfare may be very different from a residential child care worker. This is not necessarily a negative point, but both sets of workers need to keep in mind the idea that interventions can be different *but also* complementary *and* of equal value to the child.

Activity

Describe your ideas about the tasks a residential child care worker might perform for a 12-year-old child with autism. Now think about the tasks a field social worker might perform for the same child. Discuss the similarities and differences. Discuss whether you think some sources of tension might arise from the differences. Do you think sources of cooperation might arise from the similarities?

The codes of practice for teaching

Teaching in Britain is regulated by the General Teaching Councils (GTCs) and the codes of practice for teachers are defined by these councils on behalf of the various countries in the UK. Within each of the countries, the teaching profession has to some extent developed differently and has a different history. This is reflected to a certain extent in the different powers and constitutions of the teaching councils in each of the countries. The GTC in England has a Statement of Professional Values and Practice for Teachers, as well as standards which registered teachers must reach before full registration. In terms of the Statement of Professional Values and Practice, six broad areas are referred to. These are:

1 Young people as pupils.
2 Teacher colleagues.
3 Other professionals, governors and interested people.
4 Parents and carers.
5 The school in context.
6 Learning and development.

The third statement talks explicitly about working with others. The text of this statement is as follows:

> Teachers recognise that the well being and development of pupils often depend on working in partnership with different professionals, the school governing body, support staff and other interested people within and beyond the school. They respect the skills and expertise of these colleagues and partners and are concerned to build productive working relationships with them in the interests of pupils. (GTC for England, 2004)

The area of concern for teachers is helping pupils to attain the highest possible standards of educational development. Although the word *care* is never used in relation to pupils in the English standards, it is clear that Reich's notion of care as paying attention to someone's growth and development, particularly their intellectual progress is at the heart of the teaching task. Sockett (1993), in his discussion on the professional ethics of teaching, discussed and identified the virtue of care as a professional virtue in teaching. However, Fallona (2001), in her study of teachers in training, found that the notion of *care* was only specifically mentioned during one lecture. The General Teaching Council for Scotland's publication *Professionalism in Practice* (2004) does make specific reference to care by saying that a teacher is 'a professional entrusted with the care of education of children' (2004: 2). Once again, it is care as in Reich's fourth idea. This very strong idea of care as paying attention to someone's growth and development might be a helpful theoretical basis for collaborative practice in relation to a child in care.

The code of practice for nursing

Nursing in the United Kingdom is regulated by the Nursing and Midwifery Council (NMC). This professional body replaced the work of the United Kingdom Central Council for Nursing, Midwifery and Health Visiting (UKCC) in 2002. The NMC has a code of professional conduct which has seven key points. These are as follows:

1   Respect the patient or client as an individual.
2   Obtain consent before you give any treatment or care.
3   Protect confidential information.
4   Cooperate with others in the team.
5   Maintain your professional knowledge and competence.
6   Be trustworthy.
7   Act to identify and minimise risk to patients and clients.

The fourth standard talks specifically about working with others. Within the standard, the team includes 'the patient or client, the patient or client's family, informal carers and health and social care professionals in the National Health Service, independent and voluntary sectors' (2004: 6). Staff working for local authorities are not specifically mentioned. In other words this means that field social workers, residential child care staff and teachers employed by local authorities may not technically come under this section of the code as people with whom nurses would normally collaborate.

Once again, the essence of collaboration is the emphasis on the key task for nurses, which is health. The area of concern is the protection and support of the health of their patients. Unlike the standards for education, the word *care* is repeated many times in the NMC standards. The way in which it is used is akin to Reich's ideas of care as the duty to perform practical caring tasks for others, and as something that matters to the nurse. Gastmans, Dierckx and Schotsmans (1998) discussed the moral aspect of nursing and turned their attention to care. They maintained that in nursing, care is carried out through behaviours that involve the integration of the virtue of care with the expert activity of nursing practice. They said that the virtue of care for nursing is concerned with the factual concrete condition of the individual. If other professionals understand the central role of health within the code for nurses, the more likely it is that collaborative practice can happen.

Conclusion

Understanding some of the philosophical and ethical underpinnings of the practitioners who work with children is a valuable starting point for negotiating collaborative practice. It is helpful to understand the way in which care is viewed and valued (or not) in society, as the perceptions of different professionals stems from this. It is also helpful to understand how individual professionals from different disciplines may define care. In this way, common ground can be developed which meets the needs of children in care. However, we would argue that collaborative practice does not simply arise from understanding the points involved. In reality, it is much more about developing an empathy for fellow professionals and having a sense of what is important to them as people. In effect, it is about caring for fellow professionals as well as caring for children.

Further Reading

Noddings, N., Gordon, S. & Benner, P. (Eds.) (1996). *Caregiving: readings in knowledge, practice, ethics and politics.* Pennsylvania: University of Pennsylvania Press. This edited collection of chapters gives an clear introduction to the ethics and understandings of care. It looks at the meaning of care from a range of different personal and professional perspectives and argues for a rethinking of the place of care in the professions.

Understanding Organisations and Groups in the Context of Collaborative Practice

Introduction

Collaborative practice by its very nature implies involvement of two or more people. Practitioners participate in many group activities, especially formal and informal meetings. This chapter will look at the behaviour of people in groups or organisations. It is important to think about this area in order to analyse more clearly what is happening when staff from different organisations try to work together. The chapter will take a brief look at organisations and how they can have an impact upon collaborative practice. It will then go on to look at the nature of groups and how this can have an effect on relationships. During the discussion, barriers to collaborative practice will be highlighted, and ways to deal with these will be explored.

Learning Objectives:

- to examine the nature of organisations and the lessons to be learned for collaborative practice
- to consider the nature of groups and group process, and how these may have an impact on collaborative practice
- to explore the nature of change in groups and organisations
- to examine barriers to collaborative practice inherent in groups and organisations, and look at ways to overcome these.

Why examine organisations and groups?

There will be many occasions in the working day when the social worker or the residential worker has to make contact with staff from different professional groups or organisations. In addition, social workers or residential workers may have to work alongside different professionals in a group situation, for example, during child care reviews or at case conferences. On many occasions, these collaborations will be fruitful and successful, achieving the desired outcomes for all parties. On other occasions, however, the discussions or meetings may be fraught and unsatisfactory, leaving all participants with a feeling of frustration. Why is it that seemingly reasonable, pleasant and intelligent individuals can leave each other with such negative feelings on occasions such as these? One answer is that when social workers or residential workers deal with a professional from another agency, they not only deal with the individual as a person, but they also with deal with them as a member of their work group and profession, and a representative of their organisation.

Activity

Imagine you have a meeting with a teacher about a child in a residential unit who is excluded from school. The meeting is being held with a view to finding some way to help the child back into education. When you meet with the teacher, try to think of them as the person at the head of a queue. The queue consists of the same person, but with various 'hats' on: the teacher as a person, as a representative of their school, as a member of their department within the school, as a part of the local authority education department and so on. This picture is further complicated by you as the field social worker or residential child care worker. You, also, are at the head of your own queue. When you begin to conceive of collaborative practice in this way, it becomes easier to see the complexity of the task and the need to understand the various factors which can influence how another person sees their role. In the first part of the chapter organisations will be the focus while the latter part will look at groups.

What do practitioners need to know about the nature of organisations?

There has been much research into the nature of organisations. Although it is outwith the scope of this book to present a full exploration of organisational theory, it is helpful to have an overview of some of the relevant research and to consider what implications this might have for collaborative practice. In this section we will give a brief introduction to some of the basic models that have been developed in order to analyse the structure of organisations, and then we shall go on to examine the concept of organisational culture.

Organisational models

The study of organisations has its roots in early sociology. Weber conducted one of the first analyses of modern organisations and developed the model of the bureaucracy (Haralambos, 2000). The work of sociologists such as Weber was in response to a changing, industrialised Western world, which was creating large-scale industrial enterprises and large government departments, which required new, more efficient, methods of management, recruitment and promotion on the basis of merit, and so on. The early theories took a *rational-legal* view which essentially conceived of organisations as machines. Brooks (2002) discussed the development of a range of organisational models. Early theorists such as Frederick Taylor applied the *rational-legal* perspective in his study of organisations and workforces, in an approach called *Scientific Management*. Subsequent researchers began to visualise organisations in a less mechanistic way, and this perception of the organisation as a 'living entity' became known as the *Human Relations* school. As technology advanced, and new concepts became available, theorists began to think of the organisation in terms of *systems* with their defining features of being in flux and having feedback and control mechanisms or subsystems. More recently, commentators such as Lewin (2001) have discussed how ideas based on chaos and complexity theory can help people to understand how organisations operate. Concepts based on chaos and complexity ask practitioners to view the organisation as a complex pattern which, while having many general properties, can develop in startlingly different ways depending on tiny variables within its structure.

These varying conceptualisations can each be useful in helping people to see how structures in organisations can have an impact on collaborative practice. However, the key point for social workers and residential workers to remember is that influential organisational theories such as those drawn from 'Human Relations' share an understanding that the structure of any organisation has two essential aspects: the formal and the informal. The formal aspect can be described by looking at organisational charts, job roles and structure. The other is the informal part consisting of the social relationships which develop within the organisation, based on spontaneous human behaviour. Bearing this in mind can also be helpful when analysing collaborative practice. The implication of this distinction is that people may *think* they understand an organisation because they know its roles and functions. However, practitioners in any field also have to relate to individuals within the organisation and it is important to have their views of what they *perceive* their function to be within the wider organisation, and how this affects their work with other professionals.

Activity

Think of an organisation you have worked in. What were the formal aspects of the organisation? What were the informal aspects of the organisation? If you have been the member of a large organisation you may be able to reflect on the fact that teams or units within the same organisation can vary in many ways, despite having apparently similar remits, policies and procedures. Think about how two teams with similar roles and run by the same agency (for example, two residential child care units run by the same local authority) could feel so different. Discuss what you think contributes most to how a worker feels in their work environment – the formal or informal aspects.

Organisational culture

Another important concept which helps understand the impact of organisations on the individuals who work in them is the notion of organisational culture. Scott, Mannion, Davies & Marshall (2003) in their discussion of organisational culture in health care explore the difficulties involved in trying to define precisely what organisational culture means. They claim that organisational culture:

> broadly signifies a symbolic approach to organisations in order to study characteristic ideologies, language, dress codes, behaviour patterns, signs of status and authority, modes of deference and misbehaviour, rituals, myths and stories, prevailing beliefs, values and unspoken assumptions (Scott et al., 2003: 65).

The organisational culture refers to the 'feel' of the organisation, and is closely connected to the informal aspects of organisation as described above. Much of the research into organisations in general and organisational culture in particular, has focused on large private companies, but the findings are also relevant to the public sector.

The importance of organisational culture as a concept really took hold of the imagination of managers after the publication of Peters & Waterman's (1982) book *In Search of Excellence*. In this book the authors claimed that organisational culture was central to the success of the firms in the study. The significance of factors such as professional identity and occupational orientation may be one of the keys to help unlock the organisational culture within the public services. Scott et al. (2003) talk helpfully about this when they refer to aspects such as professional identity and occupational orientation as *sub-cultures*. They say that analysis of any specific work environment would benefit from an analysis of the specific sub-cultural mix.

Depending on the professional group, some sub-cultures will be more significant than others. This is a key point when analysing collaborative practice, as an examination of these different sub-cultures can immediately indicate where potential areas of commonality and conflict lie between professional groups. For example, one of the sub-cultures identified by Scott et al. (2003) above was *occupational orientation*. Occupational orientation refers to how the individual sees themselves in relation to their work. A person may identify most closely with their profession rather than their agency. Alternatively, they may see themselves as an agency person whose first point of identification is with the corporate body (for example the local authority). Yet another person may simply identify themselves with their place of work. If a comparison is made between social workers, teachers, residential workers and nurses, differences within each of the sub-cultures may be detected. Some of the issues around ethics raised in Chapter 3 would suggest that nurses and teachers tend to have a strong identification with the profession. Social workers also have a strong identification with the profession but, given their relatively new professional status and the struggle to define the social work task, there may also be a strong identification with the corporate body. Residential workers have not yet achieved professional status in the UK so may be more inclined to identify with the corporate body or even the place of work.

Activity

Given the analysis above, try to identify some points of commonality and some points of divergence which may have an effect on collaborative practice between social workers or residential workers, and either nurses or teachers, using the sub-culture of professional identity. Look at the analysis carried out on the sub-culture of occupational orientation and repeat this process using the sub-culture of professional identity as the analytical tool.

Commentary on Activity

Hopefully, this brief analysis will have revealed that groups of workers from different professions may have very different perceptions about their activity, based on the sub-cultures of professional identity. This in turn should alert practitioners to the ways in which these sub-cultures can help or hinder collaborative practice. If practitioners can identify the meeting points in the sub-cultures, these can form a common platform for discussions. For example, strong identification with the profession means that participants in the process can appeal to each other's common understanding of what this means for the young person in their care. It also means that if there is a difference, that this should be acknowledged and valued by all participants, and not just seen as a barrier.

Dyer (1985) has also explored the nature of organisational culture. He claimed that culture consists of *artefacts, perspectives* (rules and norms), *philosophies* and *assumptions*. Some of the philosophical and ethical bases of practice for different professional groups have been examined in Chapter 3, and therefore will not be revisited here. *Assumptions* are critical in the interpersonal and inter-group relationships that are so central to collaborative practice, and will be examined in more depth later in this chapter when we come to look at groups. *Artefacts* are the physical entities that identify an organisation. *Perspectives* are the ways in which it conducts its business. An understanding of the role of artefacts and perspectives in organisations may also be helpful in promoting collaborative practice, so we will now turn our attention briefly to these two concepts.

In this chapter, reference has been made to the four groups of practitioners that we have concentrated on throughout the book: namely, teachers, field social workers, residential workers and nurses. Using Dyer's approach it is clear that the *artefacts* of the four groups are quite different. However, they are valued by those practitioner groups and are seen as important to enable them to carry out their functions. Artefacts for residential workers would include the residential unit, communication logs, care-plans and informal dress. Artefacts for nurses would include some kind of health care setting as a base (for example, hospital, clinic, surgery) medical equipment, medication, a uniform or some means of identification. Artefacts for a teacher would include a school, classroom equipment, lesson plans and, usually, smart dress. Artefacts for social workers would include some kind of office as a base (for example, the area team office), a desk, computer, case files, diary and informal dress. Different occupational groups need to understand the significance of these artefacts and accept these, without making judgements about them, as they are important to the identity and task of that particular practitioner.

Once again, *perspectives* of the four groups of practitioners, as defined by Dyer, may be very different. Two aspects of perspective, as defined by Dyer, are the focus and the object of the work. In all cases, the object of the work is the child or young person. This is common across all of the four groups and serves as a powerful meeting point. However, it could be argued that the *focus* of the work is quite different. The focus for the residential worker is the day-to-day care and control of the child and young person. For the nurse, the main focus is illness and disease, and their prevention. The main focus for the teacher is the education of the child. For the social worker employed in a children and families team, the focus would be on child protection and family support. In this analysis, there are many areas of potential conflict about priorities or about how best to meet the child's need. Willumsen and Hallberg in their study on inter-professional collaboration in residential child care alluded to this when they noted that:

> The professionals working closest to the young person, i.e. those working in the residential institution, seemed to be most engaged and felt most responsible for the young person. More distant professionals were inclined to wait and see. (2003: 396)

What is required is a clear understanding that practitioners from different professional groups will have different perspectives, which need to be understood and respected, but which also need to be reconciled if agreement on a care-plan is to be achieved. However, as Weinstein, Whittington and Leiba (2003) point out, the key to positive collaboration lies in maintaining the service user (in this case the child) at the centre of practice, whatever the field may be. One of the most important messages for social workers and residential workers to take from an analysis of the constituents of organisational culture is always to recognise and build upon the areas of commonality and to try to understand and respect differences. It is argued quite strongly that a degree of insight and self-awareness into the organisational culture of other professional groups and a willingness to use this knowledge in a proactive way will assist in collaborative practice. If any proof is needed for the importance of understanding some of the underlying organisational issues which have a bearing on collaborative practice, the reader should look no further than the discussions about the failures of collaboration exposed by child abuse inquiries, as discussed in Chapter 1.

Activity

Consider the following case scenario and think about the ways in which organisational cultures may clash:

> Glendaruel, a local residential unit has been alerted by a teacher at the local school that D, a 12-year-old child in a local residential unit, has disclosed sexual abuse by his father which had taken place while on home leave at the weekend. The disclosure happened over lunch. The teacher has noted that the child is walking awkwardly and thinks there may be a physical injury. The teacher demands that the child is taken straight to a hospital after school. The school nurse has stated that the child should be removed from class right away and taken to hospital.

1   What perspectives may be at work here?
2   What problems might arise through the clash of these perspectives?
3   What common areas might be exploited as the platform for collaborative practice?

A word about change in organisations

Public services today are in a constant state of change and flux. These changes can be due to policy decisions at government level, or to re-structuring or other decisions made at local level. Some of the changes in recent times that have had an impact on collaborative practice were outlined in Chapter 1. In this section we will be looking at the impact of organisational change and how it can affect collaborative practice.

There have been several different ways of conceptualising change in organisations. Most of the research would indicate that change is traumatic but, if managed well, can have a positive impact on practice (Smale, 1998). One of the most enduring models for understanding the feelings associated with change was put forward by Hopson and Adams (1976). They suggest that when a change happens there is a seven-stage process which is akin to grieving. The stages are immobilisation, minimalisation, depression, acceptance, testing, search for meaning and internalisation.

When taken in the context of collaborative practice, it is clearly important to understand the feelings engendered by the process of change as these processes are often happening in social work departments and other agencies. Working in a collaborative way implies that the participants may have to make some changes in terms of their thinking and beliefs. Given the feelings identified above in Hopson's view, it is important to ask three questions when any change process is being implemented. Smale (1998) outlined these questions as follows:

1   Are the participants active or passive?
2   Does the proposed change alter their identity or sense of self?
3   Do the participants perceive themselves as winning or losing?

As Smale pointed out, the research indicates that change is best received and is more likely to be successful when participants play an active part in the process. They must be given an opportunity to state their concerns and feelings, and to have these listened to. They also need to feel that their professional identity retains its integrity. Finally, participants must feel that they are not losing anything in the transaction. All of this requires highly developed communication skills, not the least of which is empathy.

In collaborative practice, if social workers or residential workers are aware that changes are inevitable because of decisions being made, they should keep in mind the feelings engendered by change and the ways in which the participants in the change process can be brought along in the process. Almost as important is the need for social workers and residential workers themselves to be aware of the impact that change is having upon them, and the repercussions this may have on their relationships with colleagues.

Activity

Imagine that you are a social worker in a meeting with a teacher. There has been a child care review and it has been decided that a child (who is your client and who is currently in residential care) no longer needs a support worker to attend school with her each day. You are now discussing the withdrawal of the support

(Continued)

> *(Continued)*
>
> assistant from providing additional help for the child. However, the teacher was not at the child care review as he was ill. He is feeling aggrieved because he feels his views were not fully taken account of by the head of department who represented him at the review. How might the teacher feel about the support being withdrawn and how would you convey understanding of his position while continuing to support the decision of the meeting?

Some final points on organisations

Within an organisation such as a health board, an education department or a local authority, it is fair to say that most grass roots practitioners may only have a blurred and ill-defined sense of what constitutes the complete organisation, especially the senior management structures that exist in the larger public services. Their experience as practitioners is defined by their immediate work group. It is sometimes just too complicated and time consuming for individual staff members to get to know the organisation a whole. While it is not suggested here that this is necessary, some knowledge about organisational structures and culture are of benefit. In reality, as the organisation grows, it splits up into smaller units which become more specialised. It is this smaller unit which constitutes the work group and it is this smaller unit which will now come under discussion.

Why do we need to know about groups?

The nature of human life is that people tend to live and associate in groups. Human beings are fundamentally social creatures. Groups provide the social structure to life. They enhance experiences, help celebrate achievements and assist with difficult times. Groups of various kinds provide the context for life and, in general, create a sense of community. In terms of collaborative practice, the key groups to consider are the work group and the inter-agency group. There are also a range of issues to be taken into account when viewing the other practitioner as a member of the group. Once again, it is outwith the scope of this book to provide a full analysis of groups and group process. However, we believe it is useful to have some insight into the power of groups, how they work, and to be able to understand some of the implications for collaborative practice.

Formal work groups and their relationship to the organisation

The study of groups has been drawn mostly from the discipline of psychology. An examination of some of the more salient theories in relation to groups immediately shows the importance of the individual and their relationships. In this section, the nature of work groups will be discussed. All practitioners belong to a work group within their organisation. West (1996) distinguished between *formal* and *informal* workgroups. *Informal* work groups have no organisational identity but are nonetheless present in all organisations. These are perhaps social groups of friends at work, groups who take part in activities together (for example, sport) or people who share their opinions and perhaps lunch or take breaks together. Although these groups are important in terms of outcomes of work, this part of the chapter will be much more concerned with West's conceptualisation of the *formal* work group. The formal work group has an identity and a set of functions derived from their shared work objectives. It is a clearly identifiable entity, both by itself and by others outside the work group. The members of the formal work group have roles which are defined by the organisation. Relationships with other work groups within the same organisation are also defined. Given that all practitioners owe loyalties to the formal work group, it would be helpful if social workers and residential workers spent a little time trying to understand what the formal work group means both for themselves, as members of their own work group, and for those other professionals.

A word about teams

Within care and health organisations in particular, the term *team* is often used. This begs a question as to whether teams are different from groups, in terms of their behaviour, and whether this is something that should be considered in collaborative practice. Teams come in many varieties, and many useful analogies can be drawn from sport. It may be helpful to think of three different sporting analogies for teams. One type of group is like a football team which has a group of different people, each with a specific function, all of whom contribute to the aim of scoring goals. They depend on each other to do this, as the aim could not be achieved alone. On the other hand, an athletics team has a series of individuals, each doing very different tasks and who may not work together at all, but they contribute to the overall goal of helping their country to achieve a good placing on the medals table. Finally, a tennis team in a competition such as the Davis Cup has a group of individuals who all do exactly the same thing but whose aim is to score the highest number of points possible in order to win the trophy. Parsloe (1981), in her influential work on social work teams, likened these to the tennis team. The term 'teamwork' implies cooperation, working to common goals and shared understandings about the means of reaching those goals. However, whether it is actually experienced in that way by team members is another matter. In terms of collaborative practice, it is helpful to have an understanding of the types of team you are dealing with. Otherwise, some wrong assumptions could be made about approaches to work and communication. It is suggested here that each of the professions examined for the purposes of this book are in different types of team. It could be argued that teachers are more akin to the athletics team, while a group of residential workers are more like the football team. Groups of nurses can be part of all three depending on their setting. Guzzo, as quoted in West

(1996) feels that we can get caught up in this distinction, and suggests that 'all teams are groups, but not all groups are teams' (1996: 9). This is helpful to remember and means that practitioners need not get confused about differences. According to Guzzo the assumption can be made that within organisations we are talking about work groups, and teams are a subset of this wider categorisation. In other words, teams are a type of group and are subject to the same processes that will be discussed in the remainder of this chapter.

How groups work

As previously stated, it is important to understand the structure of the formal work group. In terms of collaborative practice, however, it is more important to understand group process. Group process is all about how groups work. It is argued that social workers and residential workers should have an understanding of group process because many of the forums, within which decisions about children are made, happen to be a group. For example, think about the number of professionals who may interact with a child and their family when they are coming into care and the number of times they meet as a group to make decisions regarding the child's placement. Some of the meetings may feel comfortable and productive. However, some may feel quite tense, even though it may be the same group of workers and the same child being discussed. Some of the tensions and discomforts within the group may be related to group process. These feelings and behaviours are normal within group process but may lead to serious misunderstandings at an early stage. An awareness of group process may help practitioners to go some way to preventing these misunderstandings. It should be remembered that groups are dynamic systems. In particular it is important to understand how small groups grow and change, and how they embed particular beliefs into their ways of operating.

How groups form

When a group of professionals come together to discuss a child or to develop ways of working together in relation to services for children and young people, they immediately become a group, and are subject to group process. Tuckman, as quoted in Vernelle (1994) described a helpful and now very well-known way of understanding the development of a group. He developed a four-stage theory suggesting that all groups go through four phases in their development. The terminology he used was *forming, storming, norming* and *performing*. Forming describes the characteristics of the group as it comes together. One of the features of this stage is a 'tentativeness' as people come together and try to get to know each other in the context of the group task. Storming describes the conflicts, tensions and battles which the group goes through before it can begin to work productively. This stage sees the various participants making a bid for their roles within the group. Norming describes the way in which the group sets it rules, behaviours and rituals, and how it defines what is acceptable within its structure. Performing is the stage of group formation where the group actually works together productively to achieve its tasks. Although Tuckman's categories are most often used with longer-term groups, some of the concepts are helpful when understanding what is happening in a multi-disciplinary group where members join each other in a number of formal and informal meetings over a period of time. If Tuckman is right, for example, then the group which only meets together once or twice to discuss a child may never move beyond the first two stages. Group process is important because certain behaviours are an artefact of where the group is at in terms of its formation, and not because of the actual task in hand or any of the people involved.

Group roles and their impact on collaborative practice

Another aspect of group process which if handled well can facilitate the group process concerns the assignation of roles. Within this process, the members of the group take on roles, or are forced by the group to take on roles. According to Vernelle (1994) group members take on two broad types of roles within groups. These are task roles and social-emotional roles.

Task roles
> Initiator: suggests new ideas or new ways of looking at issues
> Information seeker: asks for more information or clarification
> Coordinator: shows the links between different ideas and tries to draw subgroups together
> Evaluator: tries to assess the value of decisions

Social-emotional roles
> Encourager: encourages others to contribute
> Harmoniser: keeps the peace and tries to find compromises
> Gatekeeper: helps others into the discussion

Some of these roles are taken on consciously or may be ascribed by the group. The assignation of roles is necessary to allow the work of the group to proceed. In relation to collaborative practice, however, the ways in which roles are ascribed or taken on by members should be monitored. For example, the decisions made about the child may depend strongly on which person has been ascribed or has taken on the role of initiator. If, for instance, the role of initiator is taken by the social worker, their views may take precedence over the views of any other professionals and may unduly skew the discussion, unless that person has a degree of insight into the fact that they have this role, and then works hard to ensure balance.

One other role to be aware of is the role of scapegoat. This role does not emerge in all groups, but where it does happen, it can be very destructive, both to the person who is assigned that role, and to the group's purpose. As the name suggests, the scapegoat is invested with all of the problems and issues of the group and then is blamed or excluded. This helps the group to avoid issues. It is important to think about the scapegoat as they are usually perceived to be the weakest or least powerful member of the group. A power analysis would indicate that residential child care workers tend to occupy the lowest position in terms of power and status in inter-agency meetings. According to theories of group process, they are therefore most likely to be the least listened to and, on occasion, to become the scapegoat. For example, if the residential worker, as a representative of the unit, is blamed for the fact that the child is outwith control, absconds from home leave, uses drugs or any other issue, then other professionals do not need to examine themselves, the contribution of their organisation, or the larger social or structural factors at work.

Linked to this is the idea of the 'in-group' and the 'out-group'. Vernelle described these concepts and paid particular attention to the out-group. This is an important concept for collaborative practice. The out-group is quite simply a group outside your own group. The in-group will have its own set of attitudes and practices, which can lead to unfair judgements of anyone who is not a member of that in-group. This is closely tied in with the concepts of prejudice and stereotyping. Stereotyping is a process by which people attribute behaviour to another on the basis of a set of characteristics with no particular foundation in reality. A person can be stereotyped based on their membership of a work group. Prejudice is an attitude or belief which causes the person to make judgements without any rational basis. Following on from this, it is clear that work groups are forms of in-groups and will view each of the others as out-groups. An inter-disciplinary group or meeting will have representatives from their own in-groups. Within any new group which is formed either for a long-term or a short-term purpose, there is likely to be some prejudice. Most people have more prejudices than they care to admit to and therefore, as individuals, can be unaware of these feelings which may only surface under pressure. For collaborative practice to occur, the individuals in the group must try to be aware of their prejudices, especially about other professional groups, and to discard these, or challenge them, if they see them emerging unhelpfully as part of the group process.

Activity

Think about a social worker, a residential worker, a nurse and a teacher. Jot these titles down and list some of the stereotypical views of the groups. What barriers to collaborative practice may arise because of these stereotypes?

Commentary on Activity

Looking at the stereotypical views generated, it is easy to see how barriers to collaboration can arise if these go unchecked in an inter-professional group. Most of the time, if all is going well, people will not revert to stereotypes. However, if there is a problem or a difficulty (which can be expected often when working with vulnerable children and their families) and participants are under pressure, outcomes may be different.

Inter-group conflict as a barrier to collaborative practice

The final group process to keep in mind during collaborative practice is that of inter-group conflict. Some of the most interesting research on inter-group conflict was carried out by Sherif (1967) who set up inter-group conflict between two groups at a boy's camp. He found that this conflict became most powerful in the face of scarcity of resources, and that all possible pressures and power were brought to bear in the competition that followed. This study led to a range of research in the field of social psychology which demonstrated the lengths to which individuals, who are normally law-abiding and 'respectable', will go to protect their claim to scarce resources. These studies have a high degree of resonance when examining barriers to collaborative practice. In public service provision, agencies are often in the position of having scarce resources, be they placements at residential units, special teaching facilities or money to fund home care support for parents who need some assistance with their children. As such, some inter-agency meetings may have hidden agendas. For example, there may be a meeting to decide on the best placement for a child with autism. The field social worker may argue that residential school X is best because it meets the child's needs most closely. However, if residential school X is more expensive than residential school Y, it may be that the decision is made to place the child in Y, albeit inappropriately. One of the main lessons to be learnt from Sherif's research is that everyone must be clear about scarcity of resources and recognise the true basis for decisions, and the fact that conflict may arise if all parties do not share a view about the significance of resource issues in a particular case.

Conclusion

Collaboration involves working together but it is not enough to accept that practitioners will simply be able to relate to each other as people in a seemingly logical way. Practitioners are part of their work group, their agency and their organisation. All of these factors will have an impact upon collaborative practice and it is helpful for social workers and residential workers to understand some of these dynamics. It may seem difficult at times to surmount some of the issues that can arise when taking account of group or organisational factors. However, we would suggest that the two keys to good collaborative practice in this instance are to keep taking account of the group or organisational forces at work, and to maintain the child at the centre of any work being done.

Further Reading

Brooks, I. (2002). *Organisational behaviour: individuals, groups and organisation.* London: Prentice Hall.
This book is a good general introduction to organisational theory.

Vernelle, B. (1994). *Understanding and using groups.* London: Whiting and Birch.
This book offers an accessible guide to understanding group behaviour and group processes, and is applicable to work with groups of service users or with professional groups.

Social Workers and Residential Workers: The Key Collaborative Relationship

Introduction

Social workers and residential workers occupy a central place in the lives of children in care. They provide the vital human element which translates statutory duties into the reality of being in care. In this chapter we will look at the tasks undertaken by social workers and residential workers, and will explore the centrality of collaborative practice to their tasks. It is argued that the relationship between the social worker and the residential worker is the key professional relationship in ensuring positive outcomes for the child or young person in care. We will look at the day-to-day work of each of these practitioners, examine their roles in the young person's care journey, and give some indications of how collaborative practice can be promoted.

Learning Objectives:

- to examine the role and tasks of the social worker
- to examine the role and tasks of the residential worker
- to look at areas of collaboration and conflict
- to illustrate how each practitioner could contribute more helpfully to the care journey.

What do social workers do? The evolving role of the social worker

A comprehensive exploration of the evolving role and tasks of social workers is clearly beyond the scope of any single book. However, it may be helpful to briefly examine how the role of the social worker based in a local authority has developed. Prior to the 1970s, there were different kinds of social workers working in various parts of the welfare system. Having said this, they were much fewer in number than they are at the present time. They were specialists who dealt with diverse personal and social problems and had a variety of job titles such as almoners, children's officers, welfare officers, probation officers, psychiatric social workers and others. Some of these specialists were located within local authority departments while others worked in secondary settings such as hospitals or courts. The various different types of social worker were merged together when social work or social services departments were set up, in Scotland in 1969 and in England in 1971. They all became generic social workers. Some continued to work out of secondary settings such as hospitals, but now came under the management of social work or social service departments. As such, they were expected to operate within a generic framework. In England, unlike Scotland, probation officers were an exception to this rule. They were not absorbed within social service departments and continued to offer a separate specialist probation service.

The argument for generic social work was that the various social workers who had a range of titles and specialisms had, in reality, the same value base and many core skills in common. Gathering these professionals into one department strengthened the growing professional identity of social work and also helped to reduce duplication of services to families. It was hoped that if a family had multiple problems or needs that they should only require a single worker who could work with them in a holistic manner. During the 1970s social work and social service departments expanded greatly and developed many new services for children and families and adopted innovative ways of working. For example, day services were developed to offer support to children and families in order to prevent a family breakdown and reception of children into care. Social group work and Intermediate Treatment projects were established in the community to divert and work with teenagers who were involved in offending and at risk of coming into care. A great deal of energy was expended in recruiting foster carers and seeking to extend the boundaries of their tasks. However, while there was much commitment to generic work, there were also counter-pressures that led towards a degree of specialisation within teams at least in some areas. This meant that some field social workers worked mainly with children and families, and indeed in some places specialist fostering and adoption teams were set up to recruit and train foster parents. During the late 1980s, under pressure from government for more robust probation methods, and from legislation like the NHS and Community Care Act 1990, this specialisation became more marked, primarily into practitioners with a focus on either criminal justice, community care, or children and families.

In the area of work with children and families, social workers are employed by local authorities, and increasingly by the voluntary/independent sectors. Field social workers employed by local authorities are the duty bearers of the statutory responsibilities laid down by legislation such as the Children Act, 1989, and the Children (Scotland) Act, 1995. Throughout the last two decades of the twentieth century, social workers took on a major role as leading child protection workers. This work came under close scrutiny during various highly politicised child abuse cases and inquiries, starting with the death of Maria Colwell and the subsequent inquiry into her death. However, by the mid-1980s, this led to concern that the balance of their work had been tipped so much towards child protection that their role in giving care and support to families was diminished. Their interventions in this area often led to criticism for either not intervening soon enough, or for intervening too much. This led to social workers feeling that they were operating in a 'no win' situation. These trends and tensions have been illuminatingly explored by Nigel Parton in a number of publications (Parton, 1991, 1998, 2004).

The 1989 Children Act was supposed to redress the balance and encouraged social workers to work in partnership with parents. This is explored further in Chapter 7. However, the reality is that a major part of this role is still about child protection. This inevitably leads to some frustrations for field social workers, who report that they do not get the time and space to carry out reasonable support and preventative work with families. For example, Coffey, Dugdill and Tattersall (2004) in their large-scale study of social service departments in the North of England reported that the lowest levels of job satisfaction were among those staff working with children and families. When asked what could make their job better, this group of staff reported that they would like more staff or a lower workload so that adequate time could be allocated to the real needs of service users. Very similar findings were reported by the 21st Century Review of Social Work in its Interim Report (Roe, 2005). While the amount of direct work with service users appears to have diminished the role of the social worker as broker of services seems to have become predominant. For example, following an assessment of a family with a disabled child, the social worker may involve a home support worker, organise a place in a family centre, or contact a support group on behalf of parents or arrange for parents to attend parenting classes. These various tasks require highly developed assessment and networking skills, knowledge of resources and also skills in report writing. Skills in negotiating with senior staff, in order to win support for and access to the services that the social worker has assessed as being necessary for their clients, are also important.

Social workers in this setting are also guided by the overarching principle of the *best interests of the child*. In terms of child protection, this is most often about the physical safety of the child or young person, but also increasingly involves difficult-to-make judgements involving degrees of neglect and emotional abuse. The social worker makes these judgements guided by professional values but often under pressure of time and shortage of resources. In addition, they have the added pressure of how society at large views them. Inquiries into failures to protect children such as Victoria Climbié severely criticised individual workers for not intervening in the lives of these children before their deaths. On the other hand, reports such as Lord Clyde's inquiry into child abuse in Orkney (1992) or the Cleveland Inquiry (1988) criticised social workers for intervening too quickly. The issue of the deaths of children while under the supervision of local authorities is a highly emotive one, and also highly politicised. It is hardly surprising that much of the social worker's time is therefore taken up with the 'soft' policing role of making sure the child or young person is safe, rather than relationship building or longer-term care planning. On some occasions the best interests of the child may mean removing them from home and into a residential setting to ensure their safety and it is important that residential workers understand the pressures associated with the social worker's tasks, their duties in terms of both family support and child protection and the constraints of time and resources that they work under. An understanding of the social worker's roles and responsibilities by residential workers is a necessary prerequisite to establishing a respectful and constructive basis for collaborative practice.

Activity

What might a local authority's response be to the death of a child who was under the supervision of a social worker? Try to think of this from the organisation's point of view and the types of procedures it might put in place following such an event. What impact might these procedures have on the practice of a social worker in a children and families team?

Issues in collaborative practice

On the face of it, residential workers and field social workers should have a great deal in common and collaborative practice should not present much of an issue. In reality, however, the picture is quite different. The roots of the difference have been explored in Chapters 1 and 3. However, it would now be helpful to examine exactly what this means in practice. The difference between social workers and residential workers, and the long struggle for the latter to match the former in terms of pay, conditions and professional recognition has led to many tensions between these groups of staff at the individual level and at the level of social work discourse. Prior (2002) in her study of the evolution of social work feels that residential child care workers are somehow conditioned to believe that the fundamental aspects of helping or direct caring are non-professional, yet this direct care practice (of day-to-day care and nurture) forms the basis of their work. This type of care is devalued in our society, leading to a disparity in status and conditions of service, as explored in Chapter 3. Feminist critiques of social work such as those of Meagher and Parton (2004) emphasise the negative consequences of the way in which direct caring is viewed. These disparities can create difficulties at the grass-roots level in terms of relationships between residential care workers and field social workers. While it is possible to find workers in both settings who work constructively together there are many instances in which residential workers, when given the opportunity, will complain about the way in which social workers act.

Berridge and Brodie (1998) noted that residential workers reported better relationships with other external professionals than with social workers. This is a sad indictment of what we would argue is the key collaborative relationship for a child in care. A common complaint was that social workers, who have the power that goes with case management, and who are central to the review meetings did not share important information about the child or family in an open and timely way. It is noteworthy that this complaint is also often made by foster carers. Another complaint was that residential workers felt that they were perceived as a 'baby-sitting' or child-minding service by some social workers and that social workers failed to listen to them or acknowledge that residential workers had considerable expertise in the family relationships, personalities and day-to-day behaviour of the children they cared for. In Scotland children in care attend at least annual Children's Hearings at which social workers present reports. Residential workers often contribute to these reports, and could provide their own but are often reluctant to do so because they are usually seen to have a subordinate role to the social worker in terms of reporting on progress in the placement and making recommendations for the future.

Residential workers often experience frustration when social workers make little contact with a child once they have been admitted to a residential unit. Social workers in turn sometimes find that residential workers do not understand their role and the sorts of pressure they are under, not only in terms of size of case-load but also in terms of requirements to respond quickly to child protection enquiries and the completing of reports. Studies of the experience of foster carers, such as the work done by Triseliotis, Borland and Hill (2000) indicate that they will also often express the same kinds of complaints about the practice of social workers. Experienced social workers sometimes find that their feelings about their residential colleagues are to some extent 'conflicted' in that they will recognise the long hours, including weekends, that residential child care staff routinely work, and the level of personal aggression to which they are frequently subjected and have some admiration on that account. However, as research such as Berridge and Brodie (1998) indicates, some social workers seem to lack an understanding of the many roles of residential workers, and the highly regulated and scrutinised environment within which they work.

Barriers to collaborative practice can be further illustrated by examining the job titles of residential workers. There were moves in the 1980s in some agencies to refer to their residential workers as *residential social workers*. This could be seen as part of the strategy by those who wanted to professionalise the residential sector, by incorporating it into social work. However, any contemporary survey of job advertisements and job titles reveals a range of titles for residential workers, which includes: residential care officer, residential worker and other variants, but rarely *residential social worker*. This has now been further complicated by the recent registration of social services workers. In law, the title *social worker* will become a protected title, and the only people who will be able to use it will be those with a recognised social work qualification.

In the discourses around social work, these shifts in the use of language tell us something about the value of the work that it denotes. Foucault and other postmodernist philosophers have discussed the use of language by those who occupy the most powerful positions in society, and the way in which messages enter into the day-to-day discourses. These messages cloak the underlying assumptions behind the use of language. In this case, it could be argued that there is an underlying assumption that residential workers are not viewed as worthy of the title *social worker* by those who occupy the power to protect their positions, in the world of social services. If this is the case, then, notwithstanding the new registers and statutes, both social workers and residential workers must begin to see through the coded messages and the use of language to find their common ground for collaborative practice.

Activity

Imagine you are a social worker who has just placed a child in a local residential unit. You are undertaking work with parents, with a view to returning the child to the family home. Identify some of the methods you may implement to ensure that residential staff are kept informed and in touch with you. Devise a check-list of dos and don'ts that would help to inform the social worker's communication with the residential staff. If the child is in long term care, how often should the social worker visit? What do you think are the key responsibilities of the social worker in this situation?

Collaborative practice at the start of the placement: using the LAC documentation

The Utting (1991) and Skinner (1992) reviews emphasised the continuing role for residential care as a 'positive choice and not a last resort' and the need for better levels of collaborative practice between residential workers and social workers to underpin good quality care planning. They called for better assessment and provided a stimulus for what was to become the very comprehensive care planning documentation known as the Looking After Children (LAC) documentation. However, questions around the use of the LAC documentation illustrate ongoing problems in terms of the relations between social workers and residential workers.

The logic behind the creation of the LAC documentation was uncontroversial. It was designed to gather together and keep in one place all the information about a child, and in particular to keep information about different placements readily available as the paperwork should follow the child as they move. The documentation comprises a number of sections or forms some of which simply record information about the child or young person and their family circumstances. There are also sections in which to record detailed education and health status information. The LAC documentation is intended to follow the child wherever they are placed and to allow the direct care staff, be they residential workers or foster carers, to have all the important information to hand. The LAC documentation also includes a very comprehensive assessment framework called the *Action and Assessment Records,* which provide a tool that can be used by any of the professionals involved to identify key areas of strengths and difficulties. The LAC documentation also includes care-plan and review of care-plan proformas. These forms, with a degree of national variation, have now been adopted by all agencies and local authorities throughout the UK. However, it is clear that in many cases much of the paperwork is not completed and therefore loses its potential value as a tool for collaborative practice.

Scott and Hill's article (2004) about of the use of LAC materials in Scotland found that the prime responsibility for completing the LAC forms rested with social workers who often found it too time consuming to fill in all of the LAC forms. There were also issues about the speed with which a child or young person may be brought into care, with the social worker expressing difficulties about the time scale they had to meet to complete the forms. In contrast, most residential workers were usually not given the opportunity to take a central role in discussing and completing the forms, but were keen to be involved in a more substantial way. In fact, if a child or young person stays more than a few days in a residential placement then the residential workers may well be the best placed to seek out information and complete the forms. However, they were rarely openly invited or 'empowered' to do so. Many residential workers reported that they frequently received a child into care with most of the LAC documentation not filled in. This immediately put the residential unit at a disadvantage and also created unnecessary tensions, particularly between social workers and residential workers. Residential workers were motivated to gather the information for the basic purpose of getting to know the child, but it is obvious that with an agreed, authority-wide approach, that the documentation could be completed much more thoroughly if the field social worker and the residential child care worker could find a way of agreeing about the importance of the task and divide up responsibility for collecting it. This goes to the heart of collaborative practice and is clearly an area that requires considerable attention if the LAC documentation is to benefit the lives of children in the way that was intended.

Collaborative practice during the placement

As previously noted, a common complaint from residential workers is that social workers, who have the power that goes with case management and usually are central in the holding of care-plan review meetings, do not share important information about the child or family. The sharing of information is a vital component of the care planning process, and is particularly relevant to the placement plan. If a social worker has a good relationship with a unit or with particular residential workers, this can lead to valuable interaction and information sharing. Berridge and Brodie (1998) noted this when they saw field social workers visiting the units they were studying. Residential workers reported that some field social workers were very good in terms of information sharing and others were not so good. This process is not one that should be left to chance. Clear parameters for information sharing and the process of how to share information during the placement should be negotiated at an early stage.

As noted previously, there is often frustration when social workers make little contact with a child once they have been admitted to a residential unit. It may be that the social worker is satisfied that the child is in a safe and nurturing environment and that this in itself removes pressure from them to spend a lot of time on the case. It may free up some of their time to spend on other cases, which may have now moved up the list of priorities. It could also be that the field social worker makes assumptions that the residential worker will know how to progress the direction of the placement, and therefore does not need much of a contribution from them. In terms of the child, the social worker may feel that their client is now surrounded by staff and has enough in the way of professional support. Therefore, they may believe that the need for personal contact has diminished. However, reports which gather the views of young people, such as that by Paterson et al. (2003), indicate that children and young people feel abandoned and resentful if their social worker does not maintain some form of contact. Children are acutely aware of the importance of the social worker in their care planning. This is a further illustration of the need to lay down some expectations both at the beginning of the placement and as the placement progresses about expectations around contact.

On a very practical note, given the key role of the social worker as the person who holds the case, it is extremely important that the residential worker can reach the social worker by phone. This is particularly important if there are risks to the child. Part of the reason for a placement is to maintain aspects of normality for a child, and to risk assess any activities that are being implemented to meet the care-plan. For example, it may be that a young person is being prepared for returning home. An opportunity may arise for the young person to make an impromptu home visit because of an important family event. The residential worker may need to talk to the social worker about this before the visit can go ahead. If the social worker is out and doesn't return calls promptly, this can lead to feelings of tremendous anger and let down for the young person and it also leaves the residential worker in a position of having to deal with the anger. All of this could have been avoided if the social worker had left clear instructions on how to contact, who to contact if they were not available, or simply if they had immediately returned the call.

Collaborative practice at the end of the placement

As the child gets older, preparation for the time they will no longer be looked after and accommodated becomes a significant responsibility. This takes time and involves a range of areas that need to be considered and addressed with the child before they move on.

The Children Act (1989) and the Children (Scotland) Act (1995) outline the duties and powers to provide throughcare and aftercare support for young people who are looked after by local authorities. Any young person must be adequately prepared for the time when they will no longer be looked after. There is also a duty for providing ongoing aftercare. The Support and Assistance of Young People Leaving Care (Scotland) Regulations (2003) creates a requirement for each child to have throughcare planner and a throughcare advocate, and the Leaving Care Act (2000) also outlines the powers and duties in relation to children and young people who will be moving on.

Given the level of throughcare and aftercare policy and practice developments, it is vital for residential workers and social workers to have knowledge of what support a young person is likely to be entitled to as they are leaving care. It also requires that residential workers, social workers and other professionals work together to ensure that the best service is provided and the best outcomes are legislated for.

What does research tell us?

Research indicates the poor outcomes experienced by many care leavers (Biehal, Clayden, Stein & Wade, 1995). In 2002 the Scottish Executive published the findings of the first piece of major research on throughcare and aftercare services in Scotland (Dixon & Stein, 2002). This study confirmed the findings of the earlier studies and showed that although many local authorities now had some sort of 'care leaving' service, the provision was failing many young people.

Some of the key findings from this research included:

- Most authorities (77%) offered a planned throughcare programme but less than half (39%) of young people in the survey had received one. Also, 40% had not had a formal leaving care review.
- The survey provided evidence of significant variation in throughcare and aftercare arrangements. Many authorities were carrying out developments to extend and improve services.
- The need to develop stronger links with corporate and external agencies was evident.
- Almost three-quarters of young people left care at 15 (21%) or 16 (51.9%) years of age.
- A third of young people who had been looked after away from home had experienced four or more placement moves during their last care episode.
- Reliable support, whether formal or informal, was paramount to positive outcomes in most life areas and the ability to access and return to services when in need was crucial for children finding their way through the challenges of post-care living.

These are disturbing findings – though not surprising to those involved – but an indication that we all need to improve our services and practice.

Activity

Select two of the research findings above. Imagine you are a social worker and you wish to improve these two outcomes. You do not have access to extra resources but you may be able to improve the situation through collaborative practice. Discuss how you might improve your two chosen outcomes with reference to better collaboration.

Throughcare preparation and life skills development

Throughcare preparation is a shared responsibility. Research such as that by Dixon and Stein (2002) shows that this works best when the key people involved in a young person's life collaborate to support them in advance of any subsequent move from care. The earlier that throughcare preparation starts, the better the outcome is likely to be. Most of the regulations now talk about such preparation being recorded as a pathway for the young person from the age of 14 years onwards.

Ideally, throughcare preparation should cover a range of areas including: life skills development, planning for the future, seeking suitable information on resources, and establishing children's and carers' views in order to plan for and support the young person's move from care.

Throughcare preparation can be challenging. Imagination and ideas may be needed in order to create an environment that promotes the development of skills and maturity that is required for more independent, adult living. Even when certain young people may actually be moving on to other types of supported accommodation, it is still important for them to develop adult living skills.

If a young person is in care, then it is necessary to ensure that key information is provided by the social worker so that discussions and focused work can take place.

Activity

When do you think that throughcare preparation should begin? Who should be involved and how?

Can you identify the wide range of areas that young people need to develop or know about as they approach more independent, adult living?

Planning and supporting the transition

Young people can face many transitions and changes as they approach adulthood, such as leaving school, starting work, leaving home. For young people leaving care, it is clear that the transitions that they face are often accelerated and compressed in comparison to their peers who are not in care. As the research shows, most young people in care have probably faced more moves and instability in a relatively short time as compared to many other young people in the general population.

Planning ahead is vital to support successful transitions from care. Providing 'stepping stones' to more independent living can also mean that children gain suitable support and develop skills at a pace that they can manage. High levels of collaboration are needed to ensure that all children have access to a range of options as this can depend on where they are moving to, funding being made available or suitable referrals being made.

Emotional support for young people in advance of and during the period of transition is as important as focusing on practical issues and accessing suitable resources. If a planned move is taking place, young people may regress to immature behaviour or refuse to cooperate. This may be due to fears of the unknown and having to live independently after long periods of group care. During the throughcare process it is important actively to seek the child's views in order to gauge where they see themselves. Decisions should be made in the care planning process about who will provide this support and how it will be manifest.

Activity

Read the following case study. Discuss the implications for collaborative practice, when implementing such a programme. What challenges and opportunities exist for collaborative practice within this framework?

Case study

Local authorities have a duty to assess a young person's aftercare needs, ensure throughcare preparation and planning takes place, and regularly review the plans and the outcomes of a young person's aftercare support. When this is done effectively in practice, it requires a significant degree of partnership working as young people may be accessing support from a range of people.

One framework for throughcare and aftercare assessment and planning was produced in 2004. This approach is called 'Pathways' and local authorities are developing practice to ensure that they fulfil their assessment and planning

(Continued)

(Continued)

duties. Increasingly, local authorities are working in partnership with residential units and other agencies in order to carry out a full assessment of a child's throughcare and aftercare needs, which includes seeking the views of the young person and any relevant carers.

Residential workers are involved as partners in this process because it has been recognised that the staff working directly with the children and young people may be better placed to help paint a clearer picture of the young person's needs.

An important element in providing ongoing aftercare is keeping in touch with the young person and knowing how they are doing. The Pathways framework includes a requirement to review a young person's progress after they have left care. This should be done in a positive way and should recognise a child's achievements, however big or small.

Increasingly, local authorities have to record details of the outcomes for young people when they are leaving their care. This includes details of where a child moves on to, whether they have been homeless, and whether they are in education, training or employment.

Some young people may prefer to maintain contact with individuals or organisations outwith the local authority. Often young people keep informal contact with their previous carers, which can be supportive or help to encourage young people to access support when needed.

Leaving care: steps to more independent, adult living

Young people leaving care should be provided with or supported in suitable accommodation. The guidance provided with the legislation states that local authorities will want to make sure that the levels of support they provide meet the needs of each individual. Some young people will need more support than others and authorities should have a range of services that addresses these differences. Residential workers and social workers should decide who makes the contacts with future providers and how the young person is to be supported in this.

Again the availability of suitable accommodation can vary greatly between areas. All practitioners working with children and young people who are looked after have a responsibility to make themselves familiar with the range of provision available so that the best placements can be made. Some examples of steps that can promote more of a gradual move to more independent living can include:

- The young person moving initially from care to a specialist foster care service or supported lodgings. This may be appropriate to re-introduce a young person to a closely supported family environment.

- Semi-independent group living may then also result in accessing single person accommodation where significant outreach support is received, before a young person moves to their own tenancy.

Aftercare: ongoing support for children

The provision of aftercare support usually means that the young person's key contact moves from being the residential workers to the relevant social workers. Increasingly, residential units in the voluntary sector are developing and providing their own outreach or aftercare support for children who have been in their care. Experience has shown that many young people prefer to maintain supportive relationships with the residential workers who supported them whilst in care. The National Minimum Standard for children's homes in England recommend this when they say:

> maintaining existing important networks as defined by the young person, which may include the children's home. (Department of Health, 2002: Section 6.2)

The first three to six months after a young person's move from care can often be the most vulnerable period, where intensive aftercare support is often required. When ongoing aftercare support is provided at a suitable level, young people can often experience more stable outcomes in the future.

Activity

How long do you think aftercare support should continue for? What kind of aftercare support do you think young people would say that they would like?

Conclusion

This chapter set out to explore the relationship between residential workers and social workers in some depth. The quality of life for children and young people in residential care relies to a significant extent on how well these two groups of workers collaborate. The relationship can be fraught with difficulties as we have seen, but these difficulties are by no means insurmountable. By understanding some of the differences in roles and tasks, and by developing mutual respect, it is suggested that social workers and residential workers can collaborate positively to make a real difference to the lives of children and young people in care.

Further Reading

Parton, N. (1991). *Governing the family: child care, child protection and the state.* London: Macmillan.
Drawing on original research this book provides an analysis of the nature of the arguments about how to reform the child care system, and the emergence of a central concern with child protection.

Berridge, D. & Brodie, I. (1998). *Children's homes revisited.* London: Jessica Kingsley Publishers.
Based on a three-year national research study, this book explores the state of residential child care at grass roots level and compares the present situation to that of ten years previously in 1987. Using material gathered from week-long visits to individual homes, the authors draw upon their own conclusions to make recommendations for policy, practice and the future management for children's homes.

Inter-professional Collaboration: Working with Health and Education Professionals

Introduction

There has been rising concern about the health status of looked-after children and their very low levels of educational attainment. While for many children problems in these areas precede admission to out-of-home care it has become apparent that insufficient attention has been paid to them while the children are in care. The demand that social workers and residential workers pay more attention to the health and education of their charges has coincided with the policy drive towards more 'joined-up' working and the belief that the professions are operating in 'silos' that need 'breaking down'. This chapter will provide evidence of some of the deficiencies in the health and education of looked-after children. It will examine some of the barriers and bridges that social service personnel have to negotiate if they are to deliver improvements in areas which may be considered to be the primary responsibility of other professionals such as teachers or health personnel.

Learning Objectives:

- to become familiar with recent policy developments in relation to the health and education of looked-after children and young people
- to consider barriers to effective inter-professional practice and bridges that might be built
- to identify the values, attitudes and skills that enhance inter-professional collaboration.

Health

The health of looked-after children: introduction and context

The importance of good health to overall development is so central that it can hardly be over-stated, and therefore 'looking after' the health of children and young people must be one of the central aspects of what it means to be 'in care'. As far back as 1992 'Health' was one of the eight principles of quality care identified by Skinner (1992) in his review of residential care. However, the evidence shows that the physical and mental health needs of children and young people in residential care have often not been met. It has been suggested that one of the main reasons behind this includes the frequent changes of placement endured by many children and the numbers of carers involved with any one child as they move from placement to placement.

It must also be acknowledged that health services have not been very flexible when it came to responding to 'troubled and troublesome' children who often do not engage well with universal services. In particular, when social workers or residential staff have tried to access mental health services for a child in crisis, they have found that mental health professionals are frequently unable or unwilling to intervene. Hence, although children in care have had a level of need which has meant that they have become the responsibility of the social services, this same group of children have had difficulty in getting access to the health system (even though it is meant to be universally available), which would seem to be a clear example of working that is not 'joined-up'.

Case study

The Residential Care Health Project (staffed entirely by health professionals) describes looked-after children as 'Forgotten Children' (Residential Care Health Project 2004). This three-year project aimed to provide a multi-disciplinary health service to all the children in residential units in Edinburgh and their findings represent some of the most complete, though disturbing, sets of data on the health status of young people in residential care. In the initial phase of the project a paediatrician from the team visited the units and, having gained the confidence of the young people, undertook comprehensive health assessments of 105 of the residents. Her assessments revealed a host of physical and mental health problems, many of which had not been previously diagnosed. Among other conditions she found 12 young people with 'athlete's foot', 2 with 'renal abnormality lost to follow-up', 12 with significant menstrual problems and 4 with perforated ear-drums. She also found that 41% of the children had growth or development problems but only 46% of these had been recognised previously. In relation to childhood health screening the team found that 71% of the children and young people had incomplete immunisations. She also found high levels of psychological problems and in four cases felt that the problems were of such severity that an emergency referral to the local Child and Adolescent Mental Health Service (CAMHS) team was in order.

These findings support several other research studies that emerged in health and social services literature during the 1990s, among them work by Butler and Payne (1997) on medical examinations, and by Polnay and Ward (2000) on new government guidance to improve the health of looked-after children. These and other research studies revealed a large number of major health deficiencies among children who were looked after and accommodated, including those who may have spent long periods in care and whose experiences and conditions were measured in the context of them being identified as 'care-leavers'. This volume of evidence indicates the need for action. It seems clear that both residential workers and social workers need to attend more closely to the health of their young people and help them to access services. However, we recognise that in many cases this is far from straightforward due to the disadvantages and disruptions that the children have experienced. Among other issues the social skill deficits that are typical of some of the children means that they are not easy to engage with, whether in a GP consulting room or a clinic waiting room, therefore medical and nursing services will need to be offered in more flexible ways that *reach out* to this group.

Activity

Think about and discuss some of the issues involved in tackling the following specific health issues:

1   Identify as many ways as possible of promoting or encouraging better dental health generally within a residential unit.
2   Imagine you were the keyworker for a 14-year-old boy who was suffering intermittent toothache but who refused to go to the dentist when appointments were made for him. What would you do?
3   One of the 15-year-old girls in your unit acknowledges that she is having sex with her boyfriend. The staff team are also pretty sure that two of the teenage boys in the unit are also 'sexually active'. What steps should the staff team take to promote the health of all these young people, and what other professionals might you turn to for advice?

Mental health

Mental health has clearly emerged as a particular cause of concern in recent years. In one study of all looked-after young people aged 12 and over in Oxford, McCann and her colleagues discovered high rates of psychiatric disorder – an average of 67% of young people in all types of placements having one or more diagnosable disorder (McCann, James, Wilson & Dunn, 1996). In 2003 and 2004 two comprehensive studies of the mental health of young people in England and Scotland were reported by the Office of National Statistics. These provide more definitive numbers and a wealth of additional information about mental health and related issues (Meltzer, Lader, Corbin, Goodman & Ford, 2004). They also revealed rates of disorder among children in residential care of around 66%.

Quoting this and other studies the child and adolescent psychiatrist Graham Bryce summarised the seriousness of the position, and implicitly called upon the NHS to respond more effectively:

> The studies show that about half or more of this population of children have significant mental health problems; they are five times more likely than the population of children and young people 'at large' to have mental health problems. These problems are likely to show up as serious behaviour, rela-tionship, emotional and self-esteem problems. The implication is that these are children and young people who are struggling to cope on a daily basis because of mental health problems. This is a major public health concern. (Bryce, 2004: 14)

As well as noting failings in the NHS in respect of this group we need to think about why mental health needs may have been neglected by social services staff. Social workers and residential workers have been used to dealing with difficult and challenging behaviour by many of the young people in their care. However, in our experience they have usually put this down to the social and family problems they have suffered, or to problems of the care environment itself. They have therefore not tended to view the young people's problems from a mental health perspective. Furthermore, social services personnel have not usually had any training in the mental health needs of children and have been very wary of labelling children as mentally ill. Consequently they usually only seek referral to psychological or psychiatric services when behaviour problems escalate into particularly extreme behaviours. However, even in these crisis situations they have often found CAMHS teams operating with long waiting lists. In addition, some psychiatric professionals are reluctant to intervene when they feel that a young person's situation is not stable – there is a tendency for them to want to deal with the situation 'when the placement has stabilised'. Paradoxically social workers or residential workers are often turning to the CAMHS team in order to stabilise a placement that is in danger of breaking down.

The need for collaborative practice in accessing services

Research confirms that getting access to mental health services is often very prob-lematic for looked-after children. As previously discussed, different professional groups have different perspectives on the causes of difficulties, and these can be a barrier to collaborative practice. For example, studies from a social service perspective emphasise concerns about waiting times:

> Other issues raised by both staff and young people concerned the provision of child and adolescent mental health services. The shortages of, and difficulties in accessing, appropriate mental health services were dominant features of many of the interviews across both residential and foster care. (Lewis, 2000: 16)

On the other hand the mental health service practitioners often perceive deficiencies in care practice:

> Previous reports have indicated that children in care do not receive appropriate quality of health care because of frequent moves and unclear arrangements. (Arcellus, Bellerby & Vostanis, 1999: 235)

Analysing the health problems that exist for children in care and responding to them requires the social and residential workers who are the focus of this book to consider how a child's problem is perceived by others as well as by themselves. Health professionals often blame social services for the health problems of the children and young people on the grounds that there is so much placement instability. There is no doubt that foster placements break down very frequently and some residential units do not 'hang onto' children as well as they should. In England following on from the *Quality Protects* initiative (DoH, 1999) the government has required local authorities to improve the stability of looked-after children and has set a target for reducing the number of unplanned moves. Social and residential workers on the other hand may emphasise the long waiting times for CAMHS appointments, or rigid referral criteria, which mean that a child cannot be seen quickly. By the time an appointment has been offered the placement may have broken down and the child moved on elsewhere, often because the presenting problem is so acute that carers have not been able to hold onto the child. Another key criticism is that health services are offered in an inflexible manner, usually the clinic-based model. Until the recent advent of specialist LAC services, which will be discussed later, most health professionals have not been flexible enough to attempt to engage with the young person in a more familiar setting such as a residential unit.

   All this clearly points to a major barrier between health and social service professionals, and there is a genuine professional tension here in terms of how scarce resources, such as CAMHS services should be distributed. Social workers and health professionals may continue to have different perspectives on how problems should be managed but both must attempt to focus on the needs of the particular child and seek to find ways of working together. This divide is one that the government in England has decided must be addressed at a structural level, with their requirement for inter-agency Children's Trusts, with a single overall director, under the Children Act 2004 and the accompanying change programme *Every Child Matters: Change for Children*.

New developments in health services for children in care

As the flow of research findings continued the health of children in care moved up government and health board policy priorities across the UK. The past few years have seen the emergence of a number of projects with health professionals working in new ways to provide services to looked-after children and other 'excluded' groups. While this has facilitated the testing of new approaches the problem with this development is that it has been piecemeal rather than nation-wide in its scope, varying from health board to health board. Kurtz (2001) reported that in the mental health field many of these new developments have been 'pilot' projects frequently funded out of new development monies such as the Opportunities Fund or the Health Improvement Fund. Thus in recent years in some parts of the country but not others, social workers and residential workers can expect to meet 'LAC nurses' or psychologists employed as part of specialist CAMHS teams.

Case study

In one pilot project a community psychiatric nurse was employed to work with all the young people in the four children's homes of a particular local authority. The project was named the Youth Emotional Well-being Project to signify its health promotion approach, and to reduce the stigma often associated with 'mental illness'. The nurse was an energetic individual who regularly visited staff and children in order to get to know the children and establish working relationships.

Through her warmth, concern and interpersonal skills this nurse was able to establish an effective referral system and provide a multi-strand service. She worked on an individual basis with a number of young people, provided advice to staff and in other cases acted as a conduit to other health service provision. One example of work with a pregnant 14-year-old girl illustrates the benefits of a positive inter-professional culture. The girl had refused to attend any kind of ante-natal appointment no matter how much her keyworkers and other staff tried to coax her. In a poignant testimony to her lack of maturity and confidence the girl had explained that she would not be going to the ante-natal clinic because she 'did not know anybody there'. It took the intervention of the, by now, familiar nurse offering to accompany her to overcome this young girl's fear about how she would deal with such an unknown situation.

If a good level of mutual understanding and respect can be established then these health specialists may offer resources and possibilities for improving the care of the children. Given the complex and deep-rooted problems that many young people have, these specialist LAC services need to win the confidence and respect of the residential workers by undertaking some direct work with young people, but they will also have a role in connecting young people to the mainstream provision. Sometimes collaborative practice will focus on helping a young person get access to a clinic appointment or other specific health service or facility as in the example above.

Bridges and barriers to collaborative practice: consultancy

One of the most useful forms of collaboration which has been developed in recent years with the emergence of LAC mental health projects has been 'consultancy'. This refers to the situation where mental health professionals provide a consultancy service to residential and social work staff. This involves meeting to discuss a particular child and the mental health practitioner offering advice or simply exploring with the staff the behaviour of the young person. Such consultancy should be set up on the basis of a partnership approach with each practitioner bringing their own expertise. Residential child care workers need to resist the temptation to abdicate all responsibility for positive outcomes to the mental health practitioner. Most professionals recognise that the needs of young people referred to them are very acute and deep-rooted and there are not likely to be many rapid fixes or easy solutions. Consultancy demonstrates good collaborative practice with a mutual recognition of the strengths of different practitioners.

This type of service has been offered by most of the new LAC mental health projects and could involve any of the mental health professionals found in a CAMHS team. Working in the lifespace with children who have suffered great trauma can be difficult for staff and having a mental health perspective can sometimes help a residential worker understand their own, and their colleagues' reactions to the young people. In describing what they learned in one such project, the project supervisors write:

> Such children, some of whom had suffered terrible abuse, at times could only communicate inner distress by a primitive process of trying to make a staff member feel, inside them, some of the pain and confusion that the child her or himself suffered but was unable to put into words, and therefore could not work through by thinking and talking about it. (van Beinum, Martin and Bonnett, 2002: 19)

This highlights the importance of staff being able to understand and interpret behaviour. In situations where the behaviour of the young person is having a very major impact on the staff or other young people then the availability of an external consultant to help staff think through their own feelings and reactions, and to explore in a safe environment different ways of responding may be very helpful.

Such consultancy-type services are usually offered alongside direct service work where the health practitioner sees the young person and works directly with them. However, where a health professional is working with a young person in residential care there are a number of other aspects of collaboration that can be problematic, and a key one is the issue of confidentiality.

Bridges and barriers to collaborative practice: confidentiality

For residential workers confidentiality is usually offered on a conditional basis to children, often expressed by the formula, 'I cannot offer you complete confidentiality,

I may need to share what you tell me with other people involved in your care', which can mean in practice the whole staff team. Other ways this is expressed are that, 'confidentiality is held by the staff team not by the individual'. Nevertheless, residential workers and social workers usually hold a considerable amount of highly personal information about children and their families on files and sharing this information with other professionals is usually considered to require the informed consent of those it refers to. Doctors and nurses do offer confidentiality to patients, and usually do not need to tell anyone else about the patients condition or treatment, with the usual exception of the situation where the patient or someone else is in danger. This kind of confidentiality is also usually offered by psychologists in relation to the content of counselling sessions. Beyond this individual professional tradition, in recent years all NHS staff have also been expected to adhere to the Caldecott guidelines concerning the sharing of patient information. All Health Boards are required to appoint a Caldecott Guardian who monitors any sharing of patient information, with researchers, for example, and requires staff to make sure that patient confidentiality is respected and information shared only on the basis of informed consent.

Given the increasing emphasis on 'joined-up' working between health and social work personnel, and the sensitivity of much of the information that would lead NHS and social service staff to be working together, the protection of data and the nature of professional confidentiality poses problems for collaboration at a number of levels – from policy to practice. There are tensions between the need to comply with the Data Protection Act and patient confidentiality on the one hand and the need to protect vulnerable children and work collaboratively on the other. Certainly 'confidentiality' is not a sufficient reason for withholding information where a child is vulnerable. Similarly not all information held either by GPs or social workers, for example, should be casually shared even in an inter-disciplinary team. Information-sharing should be the sharing of *relevant* information, which does require the application of professional judgement. This is undoubtedly an area where there is a need for the development of protocols at agency and perhaps indeed national level in order to support closer inter-disciplinary working and effective collaboration at the practitioner level. In consultation papers issued by the Scottish Executive in connection with reform of the Children's Hearing system, the view is expressed that agencies should be required to share information to avoid 'delay and repetition' and 'to promote the best interests and welfare of the child' (Scottish Executive, 2005).

However, even if issues of consent to information-sharing and data protection are resolved at a macro-level there are still some tensions at the individual practitioner level that will need to be more fully explored as inter-professional collaboration develops. Many psychologists, for example, consider it a central tenet of their normal practice to treat everything said by a young person as completely confidential and are unwilling to share it even though they are working with a looked-after child who is being cared for by other care practitioners. In contrast residential child care workers will usually expect to get some kind of feedback to enable them to support the work that is being done, and also to help them understand how a child might react following a counselling session. They realise that they cannot expect to be informed about everything that has been talked about. However, in the interests of best practice they need to have some awareness of the issues that have been explored. In one mental health counselling service for looked-after children the counselling staff offered confidentiality to the children and initially gave no kind of feedback to the carers. However, as their project developed they began to see the value of giving residential child care workers and foster carers an indication of the kinds of issues that were discussed and gave advice about how the young person might behave following the counselling sessions (Milligan, 2004: 30). What the counsellors attempted to do was to encourage the children themselves to find some words to explain to their foster carer or residential keyworker what they had been working on in the session. A by-product of this approach was to help the children in terms of their own emotional literacy, empowering them to be able to talk about their problems in a way that they could control, and which felt safe.

This issue of information sharing between professionals both at an agency level and in relation to individual treatment and therapy cannot be fully explored here. It is an area that does cause concern to children and families, and one that will require considerable attention as 'integrated assessment frameworks' are developed and 'joint-working' advances.

Bridges and barriers to collaborative practice: health promotion and role development

Residential workers have a major role to play in promoting the health of the children in their care. We have already drawn attention to the wide range of health issues that the children and young people bring with them. In their daily work residential workers have much to contribute and with training and encouragement should be able to draw on many resources available from heath promotion staff and resource libraries. There is much that can be done given awareness, commitment and imagination. However, there is also clearly a major role for a range of health professionals to play. Health professionals of all kinds have a responsibility to develop their knowledge of the care system and how to engage children and young people within it. Some flexibility and understanding is vital whether it be the GP, dentist or child psychiatrist. Children in care have an entitlement to health along with all the children in the country. The fact that they have been deemed to be in need of social services interventions in their lives should mean that they have easier access to health services, not the reverse. Professionals cannot afford the luxury of letting different professional perspectives delay or obstruct a health service response to the acute and chronic needs that are now so widely recognised. Similarly the role of the residential worker must also include seeking out local health services, and making effective professional relationships.

Education

The education of looked-after children: introduction and context

If a key problem in health has been *access to* mental health clinics or dentists or opticians, the problem in respect of education has been somewhat different. Children in care have had access to education, although attendance rates have been low and exclusions high. Nevertheless, the majority have been in school, but many have not been achieving very much while there. Research findings, some of which are reported below, consistently indicate that looked-after children have poor outcomes in terms of gaining educational qualifications. This group of children have often experienced school problems *prior* to admission to out-of-home care and one of the first tasks of residential child care workers is often to get children back into a routine of school *attendance*. The problem is that social workers and residential staff have often acted as though attendance is their only education-related task.

While the authors of this text have no doubt that the recent emphasis on improving educational achievement is long overdue it is important that the context and the background to these children's educational experience is recognised. The figures about poor levels of attainment are often quoted as evidence of how poorly residential units are performing, and as a precursor to exhorting field social workers and residential child care workers to bring about improvements. While improvements in this area are important it must not be forgotten that for many children the very conditions that have led to them being brought into care have also had an impact upon their school experience. Most looked-after children come from deprived and impoverished areas and share the educational disadvantages experienced by most of their neighbours. When such disadvantaged children are also suffering major family trauma then their educational problems are likely to be exacerbated. A school can sometimes be a sanctuary and a source of stability for children whose home lives are turbulent, and this is why social workers often make great efforts to keep children at their school when they are first placed in care. However, if residential homes cannot be blamed for the *prior* educational disadvantages of their children it is not unreasonable to expect that children's educational experiences should improve while they are in the care of the local authority. The figures quoted below demonstrate how far this reasonable expectation has been from the reality.

Research findings on attainment and expectations

The 1990s and the early 2000s have seen numerous research studies revealing how poorly looked-after children compare with national averages in terms of GCSE or Standard Grade passes, and the numbers progressing to university have been tiny. Jackson and Sachdev's comprehensive review of the education of looked-after children, *Better education, Better futures* (2001), is a valuable source of data and complements its research findings with examples of policy and practice developments from different parts of the UK. Concern about the education of those who had spent some time in care was mobilised by a number of 'care-leaver' studies which demonstrated that the great majority of children in care achieved few if any qualifications on leaving school. Garnet (1995) discovered that 75% of all looked-after children in one authority left school with no qualifications, compared to only 5% or so in the whole population. According to Jackson and Sachdev, various studies of care leavers find that only 20% go into further education and 1% to higher education compared with a total of 68% of the general population (2001: 1).

Research studies such as these demonstrated that many social workers and residential workers were not paying a great deal of attention to educational achievement. Given the acute emotional and behavioural problems affecting most children in residential care then it is not surprising that much social work intervention tends to be on resolving family and social problems. However, focus on crisis management and basic placement plans, while justified at the outset of a placement tends to become the norm for ongoing placement practice. The consequence is that social work concern with education has been mainly focused on school *attendance* rather than on what children are achieving when present at school. Social workers 'did not place education high on their list of priorities in planning for the child or young person concerned' (Francis, Thomson & Mills in Lindsay, 1997: 9). A recent joint inspection of looked-after children's education discovered that education was neglected by social workers, and when prompted about their children's educational progress, both social workers and residential workers had an unwarranted optimism about their progress. The inspectors discovered that: 'education was rarely addressed in sufficient detail [in care plans]. Social workers and carers were often vague and over-optimistic about children's attainments' (MacLean & Connelly, 2005: 173).

Young people's views of education

In the attempt to identify the key issues in the schooling of looked-after children the attitudes and opinions of these children must not be neglected. A survey of young people in residential care by Boyce concluded that more than half of the 180 young people who returned questionnaires, 'expressed their aspiration to achieve academically' (2002: 12). This survey also found that finishing secondary education was usually the highest level of aspiration, with very few hoping to go to university. Interestingly, all of those with higher education aspirations were girls. Children in this study also gave information about factors that made education difficult for them and these included bullying and teachers having little understanding of what it was like to be in care. This theme also emerged from the focus groups whose views illuminate the Jackson and Sachdev study:

> I don't know how you deal with living in care, it is a very difficult thing. You shouldn't be treated too differently. We shouldn't be treated with any more or less respect. But the problem is that not enough schools understand, just because we live in care, doesn't mean we're off the wall.

> People have got to understand that we might be disruptive ... but it is not our fault. Teachers should realise that it is not our fault, that we are not bad people, we don't mean to do this ... I did my work [at school], had good days and bad days. When I had a bad day it was because of the night before, in my children's home. (2001: 35)

It appears that the great majority of looked-after children and young people want to participate in school and do well academically. They require both social workers and residential workers to be informed about education, teachers to be informed about their care experience, and for all professionals to have aspirations for them. This requires the development of sympathetic environments within the school and also educationally supportive environments within the residential units. Before exploring what this might mean for practitioners the chapter now makes a brief survey of recent policy directions.

Activity

In what ways might a team of residential staff create an 'educationally supportive environment', given that some of the group are likely to be capable of doing well at school without additional support while others will be very far behind their peers? Think widely in relation to aspects such as the physical environment, the structure of the day, fixed homework time or not, valuing educational success, attitudes towards education, recognising formal and informal education, and the nature of links with schools.

Government responses: targets and designated teachers

Central government policy towards residential care has evolved in such a way that improvement in educational achievement has been identified as one of the main ways in which the quality of residential care is expected to improve. The Department of Health in its Quality Protects initiative identified education as one of the indicators that local authorities were required to report upon annually. The target that they were given is that every child leaving care should have a least one GCSE. The Scottish Executive enshrined a similar indicator within its Social Justice strategy; the target being that every child should have a Standard Grade in English and Mathematics. The targets do not include achieving any particular *level* of attainment in these qualifications which range from A to G for GCSEs, and from 1 to 6 for Standard Grades. Thus the attainment targets are in themselves set very low, and are far below what most parents would hope their children might achieve. For example, most children sit seven or eight GCSE or Standard Grade exams. (It should also be noted that there are large numbers of children in residential care with significant learning difficulties and that the one GCSE target has been widely criticised for not taking account of the needs of these children to receive education that may result in educational progress that is measured in other more 'vocational' ways.) The level of achievement that is reported in national performance discussions is 'five GCSEs at A–C', and currently around 50% of the population in England achieves these outcomes. While that level of attainment may be beyond a number of looked-after children, at least some of this group should be capable of achieving much more than the target of one GCSE or two Standard Grades at the most basic level. Nevertheless, because so many looked-after children were failing to take any exams at all the setting of this target has had a galvanising effect on local authorities and many of them have developed a variety of systems and support projects to try to improve their figures. The annual reporting from every authority means that there is now more robust and complete data than before.

The first set of English figures were reported in 2000 and showed that 49% of looked-after children in the final year of compulsory education (year 11) obtained at least one GCSE or equivalent. In Scotland the results for 2003 reveal that '35% of young people looked-after away from home achieved the target of English and Maths Standard Grades' (Maclean & Connelly, 2005: 175). These figures suggest that the previous low attainment figures for looked-after children were perhaps based on small unrepresentative samples or relied on incomplete data. Nevertheless, the more recent results still compare very unfavourably with the 94% of the whole population who had achieved one or more GCSE, or with the fact that in Scotland over 90% of young people gain five or more awards at level 3 or above (Scottish Executive, 2003b).

Designated teachers

Having given targets to social work services in terms of their role as care providers the government also placed new responsibilities on education authorities, requiring that all schools have a 'designated teacher' with responsibility for the looked-after children in the school. These responsibilities include monitoring the attendance and the attainments of the young people but also acting as a 'champion' for them in the school setting (DfES/DoH, 2000). This represents a major change that should provide a much clearer focus on issues affecting children in care and provide an important foundation for improving collaborative working. It is important to note that the designated teacher is usually a head teacher, in the case of primary schools, or a deputy head or other member of the senior management team in secondary schools. However, this development was brought in rapidly with limited consultation and no specific training for those taking on the role of designated teacher. Furthermore, most schools are only likely to have a very small number of children in foster or residential care at any one time. Developing appropriate systems to monitor and support their education may take time to develop unless education authorities support these developments with authority-wide protocols and reporting systems.

Moving targets and changing expectations

Despite this high profile policy emphasis, a somewhat disquieting finding emerged in a recent survey of staff morale and motivation conducted in residential child care units (Milligan, Kendrick & Avan, 2005). Staff were asked a question about a number of aspects of work and invited to say to what extent they were currently involved in these aspects and whether they felt they ought to be. One aspect was 'involved in education'. Forty-eight per cent of respondents said that they were either 'not involved at all' or 'only a little involved' even though the question made it clear that 'involved in education' included support for homework and support for wider non-formal educational activities. Even when asked whether they thought they 'ought to be involved' in these areas only 60% thought they should be.

This kind of evidence and the continuing high numbers of young people not achieving any qualifications in their final year at school indicates that more work needs to be done in this area to translate clear policy goals and guidance into effective outcomes. Social service staff and teachers, now often working in merged local authority departments, are going to be pressed to bring about improvements in order to meet targets in performance indicators, and thus more intensive collaboration is presaged. Encouraging social workers and residential workers to pay attention to schooling is important, however, attention must also be given to the culture and organisation of residential units themselves, so that they become 'educationally rich environments' (HMI & SWSI, 2001), and provide sustained encouragement for learning, both formal and informal. Gallagher and his colleagues (2004) provide valuable evidence from one residential unit about how a 'pro-education' culture can be developed when a range of educational outcomes are identified and systematic strategies are implemented by a whole staff team. The managers of this home gave high priority to education and developed detailed policies which they expected all the staff to support and implement. Educational achievement was seen in broad terms and a positive attitude was promoted in diverse ways:

> The home believed that if the children's education was to be successful, then they would have to be adequately prepared for it, both emotionally and practically. In terms of emotional preparation, the home ensured the children were involved in discussions and planning around their education, could raise any concerns they had and were aware of the support they would receive whilst in school. In addition to this, the home sought to boost the children's emotional competencies, in key areas such as self-esteem, confidence and assertiveness – knowing that these are often deficient in looked-after children, but also vital to their educational success. (Gallagher, Brannan, Jones & Westwood, 2004: 1148)

Bridges and barriers to collaborative practice: on teachers' territory?

In the section on collaboration with health colleagues it was noted that a major change has evolved as health services began to be organised and delivered in more flexible ways. LAC nurses and others have 'moved out of the clinic' and begun to visit residential units. In contrast, in matters of education it is usually residential workers and social workers who go to the schools and meet with teachers in that setting. While a central feature of the current language of 'breaking down the silos' implies that professional groups should not see themselves as having exclusive 'territories' such as hospitals, clinics or schools nevertheless each setting has been historically shaped and dominated by one professional group. Unless they are actually based in one of the new 'community' or 'full service' schools, most social service staff will have the sense that they are crossing a professional boundary when they attend a meeting in a school.

The key attitudes, knowledge and skills that are needed when individual practitioners meet to discuss a mutual pupil/patient/service user have been explored in earlier chapters. However, the significance of the *place* where practitioners may be meeting must be recognised, as must the role of the professional chairing the meeting. Workers who are engaged in collaborative practice are likely to get used to attending meetings in the local school and most residential workers will have had experience of attending meetings in schools to discuss problem behaviour or a return to school plan after a period of suspension. Inevitably, there is a degree of discomfort the first time a social worker or residential worker meets a particular teacher and it is worth recognising the significance of the first meeting or two for establishing a pattern for future working relationships. Residential staff have had long experience in attending school meetings, such as 'parents nights', in their role as keyworkers but the focus of this chapter is those meetings beyond the routine. Workers will need to recognise the physical factors associated with meeting in a school such as time and location of meetings but, importantly, will also have to learn the roles and 'agendas' of various education staff including classroom teachers, pastoral support staff and how they each understand the purpose of the particular meeting.

Bridges and barriers to collaborative practice: raising our aspirations

Collaborative practice in this area cannot just focus on developing good quality inter-professional relationships and communication, rather the research tells us that all professionals need to significantly raise their expectations of what looked-after young people can achieve. Social and residential workers need to pay far more attention to the actual progress of the children in their care. Lack of aspiration was noted and summarised by Bullock in 1994 as:

> Generally, whatever their professional ideologies, both teachers and social workers have low academic expectations of children in care. It is believed that such children will attain little and as young adults experience unemployment, or at best take unskilled jobs. (Jackson & Sachdev, 2001: 47)

However, seven years later Jackson and Sachdev themselves concluded that, while they were hopeful about the current developments, their own research among young people confirmed the need for change in professional practice:

> Above all they [the young people in focus groups] confirmed the findings of numerous research studies that the centrality of education in children's lives, present and future is still not central to many social workers' thinking. (Jackson & Sachdev, 2001: 138)

Social services personnel need to inform themselves about the nature and structure of current examinations, and to realise that nearly all children now sit the GCSE/ Standard Grade exams (unlike the previous forms of these exams: O Levels and O grades, which were simply not taken by the less academic pupils). In the current systems the intention is that *all* children will take the exam and will be awarded a grade. If educational attainment is to be improved residential workers and social workers need to be knowledgeable about exactly which subjects children are taking, which exams and 'mocks' or 'prelims' they will sit and when these are. They need to be aware of what the various grades mean.

Bridges and barriers to collaborative practice: collaboration and confidentiality

One of the things that troubles young people most in terms of their school experience is the issue of confidentiality. It should not be assumed that all children want the same thing; some tell their peers and teachers that they are in care, while others keep it very private and may only tell one or two others. The practice of teacher involvement in child care reviews is one that has been very variable over the years; some children have one teacher who is particularly interested in them and willing to attend reviews while others would not want teachers attending at all. Some children are happy for a teacher to attend part of a review concerned with school but don't want them to hear anything of their family circumstances. In a chapter such as this which is advocating closer collaboration between teachers and social service staff it is important to acknowledge that the issue of confidentiality is a complex one. The most important point is that professionals should try to work with children in a way that lets them know when they want to share information, and seek their permission before doing so. The details of information sharing will be established at local authority level and should be written up in protocols. Teachers will rightly point out that if they are to understand what it's like to be in care, they need to know which pupils are in care. If there are specific times when individuals are being particularly affected by their home circumstances then it is likely that there will need to be a channel for passing on some level of information to someone on the school staff. That person may logically be the 'designated teacher' – though their knowledge of the child will vary depending on the size of the school. While the 'need to know' principle is useful for working out who should be told what, it does not automatically supply the answer in each case.

The quality of relationships with the child and skills in communication are at a premium here. Children understand that someone at school needs to know about their being in care. They are, however, often worried about how that knowledge will be used. One young woman, who had a very successful school career acknowledged the care of a Guidance teacher who had taken a particular interest in her welfare (Milligan, in press). However, even this teacher had sometimes left this child in an awkward situation when she had called her out of class to speak to her on a number of occasions, leaving the young woman to explain what it was about to her friends. The joint *Learning with Care* inspection which looked in detail at the educational experiences of 50 children in residential and foster care found a number of problems and made the following recommendations in relation to confidentiality:

> Three breaches of confidentiality by teachers were found which were distressing for the children concerned. Two had been taken up by the social workers and/or carer. The third had been dealt with by the young person and her friends who, in her words, 'put the teacher straight'. Some social work staff were concerned that information shared with school staff might breach confidentiality for the child. However, a number of examples were found where teachers' knowledge and understanding of factors leading to disruptive, confrontational or withdrawn behaviour had allowed additional support and positive strategies to be put into place.
>
> Other situations were found where it would have been helpful for teachers to have been informed about events outwith school which had led to a deterioration in the child's behaviour. Education departments and social work services should ensure that they have effective arrangements for sharing and using confidential information, and these should be implemented in schools and social work teams. (HMI & SWSI, 2001: 17–18)

Conclusion

There is a great deal more that can be said about practice associated with improving the health and education of looked-after children and the focus on these areas in recent policy development is very welcome. In this chapter we have tried to look at the aspects of collaboration that are needed to underpin these improvements. The role of the residential child care worker is clearly crucial to helping children in residential care maintain good health and aspire to achieve academically. However, these outcomes cannot be guaranteed even by the most skilled and committed staff. Good outcomes fundamentally depend on effective inter-professional collaboration, and being able to resolve the tensions that frequently arise when working with looked-after children. The specific practices to support a child will vary from individual to individual. Health staff, teachers and social service workers need to be flexible in their responses; different children are likely to require different forms of support in making the most of their educational opportunities. Health and education professionals are responsible for large numbers of children, and the needs and requirements of looked-after children will often seem an additional demand on their time and energy.

Therefore residential and social workers will often have to take the initiative, and will have to give time to finding out about local health and education policies and services. Where social service personnel are prepared to take the initiative on behalf of their children and young people, they can lay the foundations for effective inter-professional collaboration.

Further Reading

Jackson, S. & Sachdev, D. (2001). *Better education, better futures*. Ilford: Barnardo's.
Sonia Jackson has established herself as the leading researcher in this field, and this is one of the best one-volume accounts of the education of looked-after children. It contains a wealth of information on the legal position, summaries of research and it incorporates the views of children and young people.

Jackson, S., Ajayi, S. & Quigley, M. (2005). *Going to university from care*. London: Institute of Education, University of London.
This is an account of an action research project revealing both the desperate lack of care that some young people have received but also much more encouraging evidence of the capacity of some young people and evidence about what they need to succeed.

Residential Care Health Project (2004). *Forgotten children: addressing the health needs of looked-after children and young people*. Edinburgh: NHS Lothian.
This is the most comprehensive source of health data on children in residential care, based on the findings of a three-year, multi-professional, health project. The health professionals who comprised this team were committed to working collaboratively with education and social work colleagues and their recommendations are practical and wide-ranging.

van Beinum, M., Martin, A. & Bonnett, C. (2002). Catching children as they fall: mental health promotion in residential childcare in East Dunbartonshire. *Scottish Journal of Residential Child Care*, August/September, 14–22.
This paper provides a description of a small, but innovative, mental health project, which brought together mental health and social work staff. It is a perceptive account of the mental health needs of children, with some wise words on how residential staff can be supported and trained to help.

7

Positive about Parents: Working in Partnership

Introduction

In Britain, as in much of the developed world, there has been an emphasis on moving from a narrowly child-centred to a more 'child and family-centred' approach to residential care (Villiotti, 1995). Although their primary responsibility remains the rights, health and development of the child, residential staff have been expected to engage with the child *and* their family, especially their parents. This trend has been particularly strong since the passing of the 1989 Children Act, although recognition of the continuing significance of parents to separated children goes much further back, arguably to the 1946 Curtis Committee report. The UNCRC also strongly emphasises the child's right to a family life, and the right of separated children to have continuing contact with both parents.

This chapter will examine working collaboratively with parents in a residential context, including communication with parents, contact visits and meetings, and decision-making. When a social worker is allocated a child 'case' they naturally engage with the parents as well as the child and will often conduct the bulk of their casework in the family home. However, the focus of the residential worker is quite different, based as they are in a residential unit and working in the 'lifespace' where the child or young person is the natural focus of attention, and the parents are at a distance. Nevertheless, residential workers usually have a significant amount of contact with parents, for example, during visits to the unit by parents, or when taking children on home visits. This chapter will focus on collaboration between residential workers and parents, an aspect of practice which needs to complement that of the social worker.

Learning Objectives:

- to consider the continuing significance of birth family, especially parents, in the lives of children and young people looked after away from home

- to learn about the legislative and policy basis of the requirement to work in partnership with parents
- to consider the attitudes, skills and knowledge needed to work collaboratively with the parents of accommodated children.

Since the early 1990s social work policy and practice has strongly emphasised a *partnership* approach between social workers and service users. When applied to children in residential care this has led to a drive to maximise the *participation* of parents in the care of their children. This has involved a focus on communication, contact and participation in decision-making. This has led to an increased amount of communication between residential staff and parents, with considerable use made of the phone to keep parents informed of their children's circumstances. However, it is not just communication – parental contact and involvement in their children's care is strongly encouraged in most cases. Most contact takes place in the units where the parents have been seen primarily in the role of 'visitor'. In this chapter we will consider means by which parents may become viewed as *partners* in the care of their children and young people rather than just visitors. In some cases courts decide that birth parents will not have a continuing role in the care of their children and this chapter will also consider the work that needs to be done to keep children informed about their birth family and questions of their identity. In the past residential workers were neither expected, nor trained, to have any social work role in terms of family work. However, it is important to recognise that the issue of *attitudes* towards parents, and the potential for a role in family work, has been on the agenda for a long time, as this quotation from the mid-1960s demonstrates:

> Our attitude to parents has altered over the years too. A residential worker must at every opportunity look inwards and question her own motives and feelings. Who are we to judge these parents and resent their right to see their child? ... We now know that however bad [*sic*] the home is, it is the desire of the majority of children to go back there. I believe it should be part of our mandate to talk to and get to know the parents and so help in eventual rehabilitation, for we are the Child Care Officers who really know what it is like to live with John and Mary. (Gaskell, 1965: 36–7)

Even after the changes in the 1970s when large numbers of community-based social workers were appointed to work with families, and there was an emphasis on speedier rehabilitation, there was still an explicit division of labour; the residential workers focused on the child while the social worker worked with the family and took over-all responsibility for the 'case'. Residential teams were encouraged to welcome parents and to see themselves as 'residential officers' and no longer as 'houseparents'. By the 1990s the situation had improved and according to Hill various research studies indicated that most parents felt welcomed into residential units and were satisfied with the amount of contact they had (2000: 38). Kendrick (2005) examined a number of studies of parental contact which showed that while a significant minority had little or no contact with parents, the majority of children had regular contact and that this appeared to increase with length of placement. He also noted a study by Bilson and Barker (1995) which found that children in residential care had higher levels of parental contact than children in foster care.

However, Hill claims that although progress in this area has been made it has been 'uneven' and he considers that the most important factor in implementing a 'partnership approach is a 'persistent orientation by staff towards parents and other significant family members' (2000: 59–60).

Legislation and policy

The notion of social services staff working in partnership with parents is central to the guidance which accompanies current child care social work legislation throughout the UK (the Children Act 1989, the Children (Scotland) Act 1995, and the Children (NI) Order 1995). The word partnership is not given explicit legal status in the legislation itself but the accompanying guidance emphasises partnerships of all kinds. According to Nigel Parton the 1989 Act:

> stressed an approach based on negotiation, involving parents and children in agreed plans, and the accompanying guidance encouraged professionals to work in partnership with all concerned. The Act strongly encouraged the role of the State in supporting families with children in need and the keeping of court interventions and emergency interventions to a minimum. (1991: 15)

In fact some writers have suggested that the notion of partnership has been key to attempts to resolve the tensions between the child *protection* orientation of social workers and the child *care and family support* orientation, as discussed in Chapter 5. The former emphasis had been criticised as leading to an overly investigative approach by social workers at the expense of supporting families, while the latter approach may run the risk of letting the focus of concern drift from the child's needs and rights to the parents' needs and rights. In an analysis of how the notion of preventative social work had evolved Jean Packman said of the new terminology in the 1989 Act:

> In simple terms, the intention is to replace the double negative of 'prevention' as minimal intervention and 'care' as a necessary evil of last (and

compulsory) resort, which was amply demonstrated in the research ... with a new double positive. 'Support' is to encompass a wide range of services and 'accommodation' is reframed as a valued ingredient, to be shared in partnership with families. (1993: 194)

Partnership was underpinned by framing the duties of parents in terms of their *responsibilities* towards their children rather than their *rights* over them. Thus parents lost very few of their responsibilities when a child became 'looked-after' by the local authority. Even when the child was placed outwith the family home it was understood that the state was merely providing 'accommodation' and not seeking to replace the parent. Exceptions were acknowledged, and allowed for in the 1989 Act. There are always going to be a few children who need some degree of continuing protection from their parents and with whom partnerships with the residential workers would be limited. Some children need to be found a permanent alternative family for long-term care, although researchers such as Triseliotis (1991) emphasise the importance of continuing contact with the birth family through 'open' fostering, and indeed 'open' adoption.

The Guidance accompanying the Children (Scotland) Act 1995 has a substantial section on *Parental Involvement for Children who are Looked After* (Scottish Office, 1997, s.29–49). Again, although the term *partnership* is not much used there is a strong emphasis on involving parents and promoting what is called *contact* of various kinds, from provision of information to visits and meetings. The Guidance points out that the Act places a statutory duty on local authorities to 'promote direct contact between children looked after by them and their parents or people with parental responsibilities' (s.31). But it is not simply a matter of contact and meetings, social workers and others are also charged with:

Allowing the maximum amount of participation by parents in decision making, that is consistent with the child's welfare. (Scottish Office, 1997, s.30)

So the partnership with parents that is under discussion here is one that goes far beyond simple recognition of their continuing significance to the child. It is an approach which seeks to support the parent so that they are involved as much as possible in care practice and in the decision-making process. Hill points out that these elements in the UK legislation are founded upon principles from the UNCRC about children's rights to maintain family relationships when separated from their parents, 'unless clearly contrary to their best interests' (Hill, 2000: 57). He also notes that there is specific guidance in the Children's Home Regulations (England) that there should be space in residential homes for family and friends to visit. The issue of the amount of physical space required to facilitate good practice with parents is one that raises an issue of competing priorities and principles. Residential units have continued to become smaller, in order that units look like 'normal' homes and blend into their residential neighbourhoods. However, partnership with parents requires that units have a second sitting-room where parents can visit their child, or talk to staff in private, and bedrooms that are large enough for parents and children to talk together. During the 1980s in the era of larger homes it was possible to give over an 'upstairs flat', or sometimes staff accommodation, for visiting families. It is especially important, if a unit is used to house young people at a considerable distance from their home, that overnight accommodation is available for visiting parents and family members. Failure to provide this kind of facility critically undermines a central feature of residential care.

Diversity in collaboration

It is perhaps worth acknowledging that residential workers are closely involved in diverse degrees of parental contact; some parents visit frequently, some occasionally, and others never. In nearly all cases parental contact, or lack of it, will have a major emotional impact on the child and the rest of the group. In contrast to the work pattern of a social worker whose contacts with parents are characterised by a consistent mixture of formal interviews and short visits to the parents' own home, residential workers will be spending *varying* amounts of time with different parents in their own workspace and thus have to manage both their interactions with the parents and with all the young people simultaneously. They have the responsibility of trying to make the parents feel welcome, as well as doing the emotionally demanding 'on-the-spot' facilitation of parent–child interactions.

Residential workers also have to manage several different types of collaborative practice simultaneously. At any one time it is quite likely that a residential unit will contain one or more children who are expected to return home. In this case the staff are expected to work closely with parents to promote as rapid a rehabilitation as possible. On the other hand, *at the same time*, a typical unit may have one or two teenagers whose family ties have been extremely disrupted and who have no intention of returning (as children) to the family home but, nevertheless, retain the need for contact with the family members. Likewise, it is not uncommon for residential staff to be working with a child whose relationship with their parents is such that the workers are expected to monitor contact closely and for whom the care-plan may well be at the point of seeking a longer-term alternative family. In the latter case the residential staff may be required to record the time, duration and nature of parental visits, or failures to visit, knowing this evidence will be collated and used to support a 'permanency plan'. These all require different forms of 'partnership' working with parents, and the demanding nature of these pieces of work, not least their emotional impact, should not be underestimated. Simple exhortations to work more collaboratively with parents are by no means enough to address the complexity and variety of possible models of collaborative practice in a residential context.

Activity

It is important to recognise the emotional issues involved in collaborating with parents when one is the carer of a child who has been neglected or abused by their parent(s). Think about the range of emotions you might experience when getting to know the parent(s) of a 12-year-old child who had been physically neglected and emotionally abused by his parents, both of whom were heroin users with 'chaotic lifestyles'.

1   How would you deal with your feelings as you begin to build a rapport with the parent(s) and establish a working partnership with them?
2   What sort of supports would you look for to enable you to work positively and professionally with the parent(s)?

Why is 'partnership with parents' so strongly emphasised?

The fundamental understanding that informs the priority given to working with parents or guardians is the fact that parental relationships remain important for a child 'in care', even where there has been inadequate parenting and abuse or neglect. There are two main facets to this which must be borne in mind by the practitioner. The first is our understanding of the significance of origins. Ainsworth summarises it thus: 'The biological family by linking a person to the past and the future provides a source of individual identity, a sense of personal security, and a cultural heritage' (1997: 15). This remains true even where children have been subjected to neglect and abuse. In order to promote a child's development, their residential carers and social workers must maintain a clear focus on the flow of information to and from parents/ guardians and other family members, facilitating phone calls and visits between the child and their family. In those cases where there is little contact between child and parent(s), or where there have been multiple moves, it is vital that residential workers or social workers undertake life-story work with the child to enable them to have a clear understanding of where they come from, and to make sense of their current placement. This needs to be borne in mind for every child or young person in residential care even where there is no plan for them to return home.

Children themselves seem to confirm this priority. It might be expected that they would be quite conflicted about contact with their families given the problems that have led to them being in residential care. While it is true that relationships are often troubled it is important to note a recent study of their views which discovered that children valued the preservation of links with family, and friends (Scottish Commission for the Regulation of Care, 2004). Twenty-two children and young people in three focus groups were asked to vote on which of the 19 (Scottish) National Care Standards were the most important. They chose 'keeping in touch with people who are important to you' (Standard 3), as one of the two most important, the other being 'feeling safe and secure' (2004: 32).

The second facet is the day-to-day reality – to put it simply, 'the kids go home'. Practice experience, supported by a major study (Bullock, Little & Millham, 1993) confirms that the great majority of children return to the family home after a period in care. The same is not true of those young people who 'age out' of their residential unit at 16, 17 or 18, as we explore further below. The return home figures, from both foster and residential care, have been summarised thus:

> In a follow-up study of 450 children [of all ages] who were looked after Bullock et al. found that 82% had returned to their families within 5 years of being accommodated and predicted that almost all children will eventually be returned to their families. (Biehal et al., 1995: 82)

Residential care practice which facilitates collaborative work with parents

The notion of 'partnership with parents' builds on the long-established approach to relationships with service users that social workers have been expected to develop. The work of Rogers (2003) is still foundational in terms of counselling skills and he directs workers to the qualities of both 'genuineness' and 'empathy' in developing relationships with service users. Given what has been said about the ongoing central importance of parents in the lives of their children, and our statutory responsibilities to them, the following examples are offered to suggest how residential practitioners can put collaborative approaches into practice. While some of them may seem fairly basic we note them, bearing in mind what Hill has said about the lack of a consistent approach to parental involvement. Many of these practices are much easier to adopt with some parents than others. As we will explore below it is important that residential workers also apply these principles when working with parents who are angry and perhaps uncooperative or even sometimes threatening.

Activity

An initial admission to residential care is an especially fraught time for all concerned. Residential teams often spend considerable amounts of time thinking about their admission practices in relation to the child or young person and they also need to think about how first contacts with parents will be managed. Keeping in mind some of the principles of a client-centred approach, as advocated by theorists such as Rogers, identify some ways in which the admission process and the welcoming of parents could be managed.

Commentary on Activity

The following points of good practice could be noted.

Around admission and initial visit:

- At the first visit acknowledge parents by name and warmly welcome them to the unit.
- Prior to admission, or on admission, provide the parents with a leaflet giving basic information about the unit: address, phone numbers, name of manager, and simple rules or guidance about visits and parental participation, as outlined in the National Care Standards. Take care not to communicate this in an excessively legalistic or formal manner. Parents are likely to be highly stressed and may not retain much information, but they will remember the degree of respect they were accorded and the warmth of their reception.
- Upon subsequent visits make sure that the parent is again given the name and phone number for their child's keyworker, and that encouragement to phone and visit is reinforced.
- Have a private space such as a second sitting-room where the parent can wait, or speak to a member of staff before meeting their child.
- Give time to establishing a rapport with the parent – this is often something that workers are skilled in doing.

While many parents will be relieved that their child has been accommodated many are also likely to feel extremely depressed that things have come to this point and their sense of self-worth and self-esteem may be very low. This and other personal difficulties, such as mental health or addiction problems, which are often a feature in the families of looked-after children, will affect how they cope with attempts by residential practitioners to work 'in partnership' with them.

During placement:

- Shopping for clothes – while many teenagers will have been expected, and often want, to shop for their own clothes, residential workers can at least inform parents that clothing is about to be bought for their child and to seek any views they have.

- Haircuts and tattoos – currently many units would not only inform but seek parental permission about styles of haircut, or wish for tattoos. These are complex aspects of basic care involving the worker in negotiating limits with the young person while also seeking to involve a parent. Workers must also accept that some parents may be surprised to be asked, and given feelings of self-worth around being a 'failure' as a parent may not appear to be very interested in giving an opinion.
- Informing parents about day-to-day events in their child's life. Sometimes the parent will have to be informed about problems such as school truancy or behaviour at school. Similarly for some children the issue of going missing for short periods (absconding) is a frequent subject of staff–parent communication. Workers are also expected to inform parents about any minor ailments or visits to the doctor. However, it is important to make efforts to communicate positive aspects and achievements as well. There is no reason why the residential worker should not phone to let parents know some of the good things that have been happening, and thus to avoid the trap of regarding a week without major problems as an 'uneventful' week. Steady attendance at school and good behaviour should also be subjects worthy of communication with a parent.

The agency and unit manager's role:

- Make partnership with parents an explicit part of the unit Statement of Purpose.
- Encourage parents to support each other and share experiences; there have been attempts to get parents together in groups in order to both empower them and to gain their views, although as Quinn (2000) reports these have been rare. As units have become smaller it is difficult to see how individual units could hope to establish any kind of parental group but there is no reason why authorities should not seek to do so on in relation to parents of children in a number of different units.
- Develop parent satisfaction measures, perhaps by devising questionnaires to encourage parents to express their views about the care process and their views of their child's experience.

Rehabilitation and shorter-term care

Residential workers can play a major role in supporting children and their parents to overcome the problems that have led to an admission to care. However, they need to recognise how varied the responses of parents may be to the communications they receive from workers. For example, parents of a looked-after child are likely to have had contacts or meetings with quite a number of workers and may have difficulty sorting out the seniority and respective roles of social workers, senior social workers, residential keyworkers and managers, educational psychologists and so on. It does bear emphasising that the majority of children admitted to residential care return at some stage to the parental home, and the key role of all social service staff is to do everything they can to strengthen that bond while maintaining focus on the child's needs and rights. This includes their rights to protection and to having their views heard and taken seriously, and of course some children do not want to return home. It is important to understand that parents lose very few of their parental rights and responsibilities when their child initially becomes 'looked-after'. Residential workers while empathising with the child or young person, also need to work hard to empathise with parents themselves, many of whom will be feeling very upset and embarrassed about their children being 'in care' and are likely to be dealing with many problems in their own lives. Many parents find that they can relate well to residential workers where they are warmly received and shown respect. Parents also have a significant role to play in the formal care-planning and reviewing process and if a child is in care for an extended period it is likely that the residential workers will have a major role to play, jointly with the field worker, in maximising the parents' participation in the care-planning process.

Residential workers also have much to contribute to the rehabilitation process in their direct work with the young person. In many cases children are entering care from a family which includes a step-parent. Research demonstrates that relationships with step-parents may be especially fraught (Visher & Visher, 1987; Papernow, 1993). Stevens examined some of the figures for one residential service and found that 'over 60% of referrals were from young people in step-families' (2000: 117). Residential workers may well have to manage the emotions of the young person and the arrangement of contacts and visits where the young person has a very difficult relationship with a step-parent, or co-habitee of their mother/father. Similarly, experienced residential workers know how difficult contact can be with a long-absent father (or mother) whom a child has 'idealised' for some years. Some residential workers have considerable interpersonal skills, built up over years of contact with families, which allow them to achieve a great deal of progress with parents and children. However, there are few units which are staffed to provide a regular level of family work, or 'outreach', or aftercare as this kind of work is variously known.

Family contact with children in longer-term care

Maximising family contact is self-evidently vital where rehabilitation is the goal. It is argued here that even where a child is in longer-term care, while contact may be less intensive, collaborative working should still characterise the relationship between care staff and parents. It is especially important that relationships with other family members are not neglected. The birth family remains of great significance to children who have lived in care for a number of years and who become 'care-leavers' at the age of 17 or 18. Many of them will look to their parent(s) and other family members for practical and emotional support and some of them are driven to discover if there might still be a place for them in the family home. The research of Biehal and her colleagues (1995), although only based on a sample of 74 young people provides some of the most detailed examination of these issues. Similar figures have been reported in a more recent Scottish survey (Dixon & Stein, 2002). Biehal et al. found that only 12% of care-leavers returned directly to parents or family directly from residential or foster care, and added that:

> Even if we include those who stayed for brief periods of time, ... the proportion of care-leavers who returned to their families for any period of time at all in the first nine months of leaving care rises only to 36% of the sample. (1995: 38)

They did find, however, that many more made regular visits and some found that previously poor relationships improved:

> Although very few were reunited with their families, the majority (81%) did have some contact in the early months of leaving care, and two thirds saw family members at least weekly at this stage. (1995: 83)

The lessons that can be drawn from this are that better managed contacts between teenagers and parents will help the transition from residential care. Better and more sophisticated management of links between teenagers and parents, associated with counselling of the young people about their relations with their parents, their hopes and fears, would help some young people dispel unfounded hopes or myths about their place in the family. It would also help them think more realistically about their own needs as they move towards finding a place to live, a social network and a set of goals and aspirations. Too often it has been discovered that young people, who have spent time in care, deal with their fears for the future by investing, understandably but often unwisely, in hopes that they will be able to put things right and return home when they have left care. Fundamental to this better management of home links around the time that young people move on from group (or foster) care is the need for social work agencies to provide much greater commitment to these young people and more appropriate forms of residential care or supported living for them. The recent Children (Care Leaving) Act 2000 for England and Wales, and the Regulation of Care (Scotland) Act 2001 extended the duties on local authorities to take more responsibility for this most vulnerable section of the population – and stop the process of ejecting young people from residential and foster care at 16 or 17 years of age. The Regulations are explicit:

> The general principle is that young people should continue to be looked after until 18, if it is in their best interest, and this guidance should be read with that principle in mind. (Scottish Executive, 2004b, 1.3)

The legislation throughout the UK requires that all young people have a care-leaving plan and a named worker to monitor the plan and provide them with support.

Research and good practice indicate that it is in the interest of the young people in longer-term care for them to be helped to maintain regular contact with their parent(s) and other family members and it is likely that the care-plan for every child or young person will include a section which deals with their family links. Nevertheless, residential workers need also to recognise that parents in this situation may feel discouraged and despondent about making the effort to keep regular visits going, especially if it means visits to the unit rather than home visits by the child. Each family situation is different but if workers recognise both the importance and the difficulties of maintaining regular contact, they can explore different kinds of contact, and should look to help young people and their parents negotiate an acceptable pattern of contact. Teenagers can initiate contact themselves, and it does not all need to be arranged by staff but most families will probably gain from having a skilled intermediary who can prompt regular contact and help each party maintain engagement with the other. Workers should be aware of normal adolescent development including the fact that teenagers often do not talk much to their parents, even when living in the same house – famously represented by the monosyllabic and taciturn teenager 'Kevin' in the Harry Enfield comedy sketches.

Activity

Reflect on your own experience of parenting, and possibly that of others who are well known to you. (This is likely to be much easier for those who have become parents themselves, and are sometimes shocked to discover that in certain situations they hear themselves talking to their children as their parents talked to them!) Erikson (1959), when exploring the development of identity within the life cycle, characterised adolescence as the time of 'identity versus role confusion'. It is a stage often characterised, from an adult perspective, as a time of rebellion; either against parental guidance and norms and/or societal or cultural conformity. One of the challenges facing direct care workers (and foster-parents) is to try to distinguish between what might be considered as 'normal' rebellious behaviours and behaviours which are more to do with distress associated with loss of family ties, mental health problems and fears for the future.

1   Try to identify times when your relationship with your parent(s) was strained. When did things begin to improve and why?
2   At what age and stage of life did you leave home (if you have done so), and what degree of contact have you since had with your parents?

It's not just parents

While this chapter has focused on the central relationship of parent(s) and child, each young person also needs to have continuing contact with other members of their family. Discovering who the important members of the wider family are is thus a key professional task. Commonly one child from a family becomes 'accommodated' but sometimes sibling groups are admitted at the same time. Keeping sibling groups together is well recognised as good practice; however, it appears that the shortage of placements and limits on bed numbers in both foster and residential homes means that in practice children are often separated from siblings. As these are the longest lasting relationships that most people have, as well as some of the closest, maintaining these links is important too. Beyond the immediate nuclear family it is also likely that each young person will have extended family members who are concerned about them. It is true that the families of children who end up in residential care may have suffered many estrangements, and grandparents, aunts and uncles may have had bad relationships with parents prior to a child becoming accommodated. Even where relationships are reasonable they may not be sure how to go about expressing their familial ties, and look to the social work and residential staff to reach out to them.

Another feature of the families of children in care is that many come from single-parent families and it is important, even if there is an absent parent, that some efforts be made to discover who they are and to explore at least whether they are willing to engage with their child over a period of time. If relationships were strong, then it is likely that the social worker would have explored that option and have worked towards placing the child with the 'other' parent, so it is likely that in practice bonds may well have been weak or weakened over a long time prior to admission, but nevertheless some information and contact should be explored.

Supervising contact – the most uncomfortable role?

In the great majority of cases residential workers are expected and encouraged to promote as much contact as possible between looked-after children and their parent(s) or guardians. However, in a small number of cases courts decide that children in care need protection from their parents even during relatively short visits. Such protection is required either because the parents will seek to deliberately mistreat the child, including threatening him or her, for example, in the case where there may be court proceedings for child abuse. Sometimes children and young people also need protection from a parent who may mean no harm but whose emotional or psychological state means that they may provoke stress or distress in the child by the way they behave or the things they say. In situations such as these the parents normally still have the parental rights and responsibilities and will in general terms be free to exercise their right to see and speak to their child. Nevertheless, because of the need to protect children, the courts or Children's Hearing in Scotland, may determine that conditions are applied to visits by parents, and these conditions may include the provision that the parent should have no unsupervised access to the child.

There are a variety of ways and locations in which contact between parents and children may be supervised. Sometimes children and parents may be taken by social services staff to a specially designated 'contact' centre or place with comfortable rooms, tea and coffee facilities and sometimes toys and games. In these places there will be regular staff whose job it is to stay with the parent(s) and child while contact is taking place. They will keep the interactions and conversations of the parent and children under direct observation. They will be expected to intervene if they feel that the actions of the parent are inappropriate. This kind of direct physical supervision of contacts between parent and child can also take place in the residential unit and in these circumstances it often falls to the residential worker to undertake the supervision. This can be an uncomfortable role as workers may naturally have some sense of discomfort at intruding on private conversations of the most personal kind. Even if they have concerns about the possible harm the parent may do to the child, most residential workers are likely to feel sorry for a parent who finds that their greetings, hugs and intimacies with their child are being watched by another. Uncomfortable or not this is an important role, and through experience workers learn to manage their own discomfort and carry out their duties in the most appropriate manner. The supervising worker will usually sit in a corner of the room as far away as is compatible with actually keeping all of the family members in view. On the first occasion of a supervised contact the worker should, of course, introduce themselves to the parents if they are not already known to them, and then explain how this supervision will be carried out. The parent is very likely to be nervous and uncomfortable and it may seem that explaining things to them will not achieve much. Nevertheless, it is important that the residential worker explains their role. Any worker in these circumstances must also be clear about what is expected if the parent behaves in an unacceptable way, if the child appears to be becoming upset or if they leave the room.

Keys to effective collaboration: values, attitudes and skills

It has been noted how the guidance associated with the various Children Acts and Orders emphasises the ways in which the parents of children who are accommodated away from home are expected to be involved in the care of their children. These are challenging tasks to follow through and there must always be some danger that residential workers will focus on the day-to-day care issues at the expense of parental involvement which may become rather superficial or even tokenistic in nature. While the residential worker is mainly concerned about working with the child or young person, it is important for the child's sake that the residential practitioner also works hard to understand and empathise with the parent and to negotiate with them in a respectful way. However, it is also very important to recognise the power differentials that are at work in a relationship between a keyworker and a parent. As we have commented previously residential workers do not feel that they have much professional power; they may feel that how they work is so constrained by procedures that they have little autonomy or sense of empowerment. Nevertheless, the residential worker should recognise that they have a great deal of power in relation to the parent of a child in care. Not only have they (and their colleagues) taken over the care of the child but they also represent the local authority and ultimately the state. Therefore workers need to develop an objective view of the professional power they have or share as employees of a child care agency, and take account of it as they build relationships with parents and other family members. Adopting a positive commitment to working in an inclusive and participatory way with a parent requires imagination, persistence and the capacity to deal with a range of different responses or emotional states that are likely to characterise many of the parents' interactions.

A productive and empathetic relationship between a residential worker and a parent requires the former to be willing to separate out how the parent presents and what they may be feeling (Pilkington, 2006). Some parents have an 'angry' disposition and have a tendency to confront professionals involved in the care of their child. Their aggression may stem from a feeling that their understanding of their child is not being fully considered and they may object to their knowledge being ignored or questioned. However, their level of aggression may be an indicator of their frustration with the system rather than the unit itself. Their anger may also be bound up with feelings of inadequacy, frustration and helplessness. As Gascoigne (1995) has pointed out in terms of the relationships between teachers and parents of children with learning disabilities, if professionals are not able to acknowledge and attempt to understand parental feelings and only respond to the surface behaviour, then the risk of the partnership arrangements breaking down are high.

In a similar way some parents may present as quite distant or 'uncaring' about their child. The difficulties the parents themselves may be experiencing are often so significant that they can appear to have little time for their child's difficulties. In this situation the negative parental attitude may be seen by professionals as a causative factor in their child's difficulties, and in some cases this will be so. However, many parents may simply be overwhelmed or afraid of the social work system, or have such low expectations of what the system can offer them or their child. Such people may not wish to work in collaboration and feel that there is no point in actively engaging with professionals. There are other parents who seem to be very willing to go along with almost anything that professionals suggest – the acquiescent or submissive parent. In a sense these are an easy group to work with as they readily comply with requests though they rarely offer their opinions spontaneously. This does not mean that they do not have opinions and the worker has to make the effort to go beyond an acquiescent relationship which may be based on the fact that the parent has lost confidence in their own contribution to the child's welfare.

In all of these different situations the residential worker needs to proceed with an openness and respect which indicates acceptance of what a parent might be saying. They also need an understanding that the parent of a looked-after child is likely to be experiencing a cauldron of emotions and so it is vital to look beyond the immediate behaviour and to consider how they may be feeling.

Conclusion

This chapter has suggested that seeking to work collaboratively with parents will take various forms and can be challenging. Nevertheless, there are many ways in which residential practitioners can build relationships with the parents of the children and young people in their care, and much that can happen in practice to promote a working relationship. Promoting such relationships is important to underpin rehabilitation, but even when there is no plan for the child to return home, parental contact is beneficial for the child's identity, security and development into adulthood. Even for those children in long-term care who have little or no contact with their birth parents it is important that they have information about their parents and family members, and as clear a picture as possible of their life-story. All of this means that the residential worker must maintain a focus on parents, siblings and the wider family as well as the child; they must be 'child-centred' but recognise that each child is part of a family.

Further Reading

Hill, M. (2000). Inclusiveness in residential child care. In M. Chakrabarti and M. Hill (Eds.), *Residential child care: international perspectives on links with families.* London: JKP, pp. 31–6.
An excellent summary which brings together a wealth of research findings and explains the evolution of the partnership approach to care practice.

Packman, J. (1993). From prevention to partnership: child welfare services across three decades. *Children & Society,* 7(2), 183–95.
This article focuses on policy development, and sets the current emphasis on partnership in the context of prevention – an important but often ambiguous concept. It has often been noticed that many social workers appear to view preventing admission to care as identical to preventing family break-up.

Collaborating with Children and Young People

Introduction

The articles of the United Nations Convention on the Rights of the Child (UNCRC) describe the rights of children to *provision* of the necessities for healthy development and *protection* from danger and exploitation, but also emphasise the rights of young people to *participation*. For many years child care legislation and guidance has stressed the importance of consulting young people in terms of their care-plan and at review meetings; however, in recent years some agencies and workers have been attempting to strengthen the participation of young people in all aspects of their care experience, whether it be the day-to-day life in the home or in formal decision-making meetings. In this chapter therefore we will often use the term *participation* rather than *collaboration* in examining how workers can work *with* the children and young people in their care.

Learning Objectives:

- to consider the changing place of children in society
- to explore children's rights as expressed in the UNCRC
- to explore how rights to participation may be promoted by those working with children in residential care.

The social construction of childhood

> In the variety of social settings children experience, they may find their competence unacknowledged and their viewpoints overlooked or ignored; they are understood to be unreliable commentators on their own lives. (Foley, Roche & Tucker, 2001: 6)

In this section, the shifting realities of childhood, and the development of ideas about the place of children in society will be considered. It is recognised that the pheno-menon of the teenager emerged, at least in the more prosperous western societies, in the years after the Second World War and was associated with increasing prosperity and spending power on the one hand and on the other the emergence of a 'youth cul-ture' that was more distinct from the world of adults than ever before. In recent times commentators such as Lindstrom & Seybold (2004) have raised issues about the effects of increased spending power in the hands of younger children and the devel-opment of children's culture, with the emergence of extensive markets in products aimed at children, including music, fashion and TV programmes.

Our understanding of what a child is, and what the boundaries of childhood are, is often taken for granted, and it is perhaps easy to assume that childhood has been defined in a similar way throughout history. However, it should be recognised that childhood is not just a biological stage. The definition and boundaries of the child have not always been seen in the same way. Our understanding of childhood is con-structed or understood differently in different cultures and eras. By drawing on the ideas of Berger & Luckman (1967) about the social construction of reality we can see that much of what people think of as the universal characteristics of childhood is in fact shaped by their own particular society and culture and informed by the images that surround them in the mass media.

Aries (1962) suggested that the notion of childhood has significantly changed over the centuries. He argued that in the medieval period, once children were six or seven years old, they joined the world of adults and did not have a separate domain of social life. In effect, they did not have an extended childhood as it is commonly understood in modern Western society. He argues that in the main they joined the adult world as workers, helping their parents in whatever their work was, being dressed in similar types of clothes, eating the same food, and even fighting and going to war alongside their parents. In one of his most original ideas he suggested that evi-dence about how children were perceived could be gleaned from paintings from dif-ferent eras. He suggested that in the Middle Ages children were often depicted with similar facial features to adults and that only their size was different, in other words that they were being seen as 'mini adults'. He postulated that as new ideas of child-hood emerged, such as the pure or innocent child in the writings of Rousseau and others, the world of the child became increasingly differentiated from the adult world. This process has continued and evolved into the contemporary situation where childhood within Western society has been increasingly extended. Subsequent writers have critiqued the ideas of Aries (for example, Pollock, 1983), but his think-ing opened the way for a much deeper analysis of children's experiences and the emergence of a distinct sociology of childhood, for example, in the work of researchers such as Brannen & O'Brien (1995), and James, Jenks & Prout (1998).

Commentators such as Hendrick (2003) argue that children have often been con-structed as either potential victims, in need of care and protection, or as potential threats, in need of control and restraint, rather than as whole persons. They are also often seen as adults in waiting rather than as subjects in their own right, such as when spending on education is advocated for in terms of preparing children and young people for the world of work. In this context children are seen primarily as an *investment*. These themes can be discerned in the way many political and professional concerns about children and young people are expressed. For example, in recent years many child care professionals have become concerned about the particular emphasis in government policy on tackling youth disorder, 'yob culture', and the issue of persistent offenders and the threat they pose to the wider community. It is argued here that children in residential care are particularly vulnerable to negative constructions of their identity because of the stigma surrounding residential care, and by virtue of the process of 'labelling'. In sociological terms, labelling theory was first advanced by Becker (1963) in his discussions of deviance. Labelling theory proposes that society creates both formal and informal sets of rules and rituals, which people must adhere to in order to be accepted as members of that society. These rules include quite subtle injunctions which can strongly influence specific aspects of behaviour that might be thought of as personal and individual, such as the way an individual chooses to dress. Differences, or deviancy in one aspect of behaviour can result in negative labels being attached to those who do not conform to these expectations or 'rules'. For a child in care, the individual personality and particular issues of the young person may be subsumed under what Becker would refer to as the *master label* of their status in residential care. From this perspective children in residential care are particularly prone to being seen as mainly as victims or villains which, in both cases, can lead to the desire to want to do something *to* them, or to 'fix' them. Such a process may lead those professionals who work with children in care to disregard the positive aspects of the child's character and personality, and perhaps to ignore or underestimate the contribution which children themselves can make. For example, Emond (2003) in her unique ethnographic study of young people in care discovered that this group often provide each other with a great deal of support which was often disregarded by the residential workers. So, while seeing the child in terms of an 'investment' may seem less harmful than seeing them as villain or victim, it is important that children are not evaluated mainly in terms of their future potential either. Rather from the point of view of participation, children should be viewed as actors who can determine their own lives in the present. This point is important for practitioners because, unless the practitioner goes beyond the presenting problems and respects the child's strengths and abilities, any degree of participation is likely to be, at best, tokenistic and at worst, meaningless.

This tendency to see the child primarily as an object who needs something (or many things) done *to* them can be further exacerbated in the case of disabled children. The basic rights and needs of disabled children are no different from those of any other child and their disability simply means that their needs may have to be met in a different way. However, the predominant *constructions* of disability are such that disabled children are almost always seen as dependent rather than capable, and passive rather than active subjects. Marchant (Foley et al., 2001) reported that disabled children tend to experience exclusion in all areas of life and especially when it comes to decision-making, and this may be perpetuated, even in a care setting if, workers do not believe that children with disabilities do have views and opinions that can be discovered. Hawthorn (2005) has pointed to the ways in which staff in residential care can promote participation when they adopt a commitment to communicating with disabled children, including those with very limited or absent verbal communication.

A history of children's rights

The concept of children's rights has a longer history than is sometimes recognised. The first formal international statement came in 1924 with the Declaration of Geneva, endorsed by the League of Nations which said that children have a right to care and protection. In 1959 the General Assembly of the United Nations adopted a second Declaration on the rights of the child, which began to extend the concept of rights, including specific rights such as the right of the child to have a name and nationality from birth. However, this declaration was not binding on UN members and did not have a procedure for implementation.

During the International Year of the Child in 1979, Poland proposed a Convention on the Rights of the Child. That Poland should have a leading role in the history of children's rights is due in significant measure to the work and character of a remarkable man called Janusz Korczak; someone not widely known within child care in the UK. Korczak was a Jewish paediatrician and a leading figure in child welfare in pre-war Poland. He was the director of two children's orphanages in which he developed many humane and innovative practices, involving the children in many aspects of the care and the rules of the homes. This involved setting up a children's 'parliament' and 'courts'. These 'courts' had child judges and any child in the orphanage with an issue could take it to the court. Even the adults had to submit to its judgements. Korczak was not particularly impressed by the declaration of Geneva: 'Those lawgivers confuse rights with duties. Their declaration appeals to goodwill, when it should insist. It pleads for kindness, when it should demand' (Joseph, 1999). As the Nazi regime pursued its 'final solution' Korczak, declining offers of help to escape, accompanied the children from the Jewish orphanage when they were taken to the Warsaw ghetto. He stayed with them when, along with many others, they were transported to the Treblinka concentration camp where he died. Korczak said that he needed to accompany these children so that they did not lose trust in all adults. The International Year of the Child in 1979 was also named the Year of Janusz Korczak by UNESCO.

Defending children's rights in practice is not without its problems, however. For example, when discussing children's rights with professionals who spend much of their working day with children, such as teachers or residential workers, there is a tendency among some to adopt a somewhat defensive approach, characterised by statements such as 'What about our rights?' It is also true that sometimes children will try to justify 'bad behaviour' by claiming their rights to make personal choices. However, such claims do not invalidate the existence of rights, rather this challenge has to be met in terms of an accurate understanding of rights; namely, that children (like adults) do not have the right to do whatever they want, and cannot justify actions which violate the rights of others. Another defensive response that is commonly made is that children should not just be informed about their *rights* but that, at the same time, they should also be made aware of their *responsibilities*. However, rights are not dependent on responsibilities in this way. Rights are by definition an entitlement and not dependent on good behaviour or 'being responsible'. It is true that no one can claim a right for themselves that undermines the rights of others, rather everyone has the responsibility to respect the rights of others, as argued and practised by Korczak.

Poland's proposal for a specific convention for children generated debate around the notion that children have independent human rights, and how these might be advanced. Following the initiatives of 1979, a working group was set up to discuss how this could be developed. Ten years later, on the 20 November 1989, the UN General Assembly adopted the UNCRC. In 1991 the British government ratified the UNCRC, thus committing the UK to implementing and making a reality of these rights. It has now been ratified by all countries with the notable exception of the USA. The UNCRC sets some universal standards for the way in which children should be regarded and the manner in which their rights are to be respected. The articles in the UNCRC are grouped around four basic principles. These are as follows:

1   **Non-discrimination**   The UNCRC applies equally to all children, everywhere.
2   **The best interests of the child**   In all matters concerning children, their best interests should prevail.
3   **Survival and development**   Priority should be given to ensure that the rights of children to survival and development are fully respected.
4   **Participation**   Children should have the opportunity to be heard and to have their opinion taken into account in decisions that affect them.

For the purposes of this chapter, this fourth principle is particularly relevant and should underpin the collaborative activities of all professionals in residential child care.

The UNCRC and the right to participation

As we have noted, social policy for children in Western society is based to a considerable extent on a view of children as dependent. Although the situation in the UK is improving with the appointment of Children's Commissioners, the wider view of the population at large tends to lag behind these innovations. Adults, and in particular those who have a professional interest in children, often claim to know what is best for them. It is almost as if the old adage that children should be 'seen and not heard' still operates in many circumstances. However, the UNCRC guarantees children the right to participation: *the right to express themselves and be heard in all matters affecting them*. This is particularly important in legal proceedings affecting children in residential child care, where they may be involved as victim of a crime, a witness or an offender, and also in social work proceedings such as child care reviews. The UNCRC, however, also says that the age and capacity of the child to express his or her views should be properly assessed and taken into consideration. While very young children will only have a limited capacity to express views and preferences it is important that this qualification, about 'age and capacity', should not be used as an excuse to deny young people their own voice, or to speak for them in an unthinking way. The UNCRC is quite explicit in this regard and places a responsibility on those working with children to give them a real voice which should be respected and taken seriously.

The UNCRC in UK legislation

Although the UK has signed the UNCRC, such international treaties are not automatically incorporated into UK legislation, and in themselves they do not have the same force of law as parliamentary legislation. In the case of the UNCRC it means that no one can actually go to court to challenge the government on the basis of failure to act on a specific article, and further there is no 'International Court' for children's rights. However, a United Nations Committee on the Rights of the Child does monitor what governments are doing in relation to the Convention, and it visits each signatory country and produces a five-yearly report on the extent to which they are complying with the Convention (UNCRC, 2002). Since the UNCRC was ratified in the UK, it has increasingly influenced new legislation and child care policy, notably through the Children Acts.

The Children Act (1989), the Children (Scotland) Act (1995), and the Children (Northern Ireland) Order 1995 are currently the primary legislation for children in England and Wales, Scotland and Northern Ireland respectively. The key principles of these Acts draw upon the principles and concepts of the UNCRC, and they all make specific mention on the responsibility of the authorities to seek the views of the child. It is also important to note here the existence of the European Convention on Human Rights (ECHR) which applies to all citizens including children. In 1998 the Human Rights Act incorporated the ECHR into UK law. This directly supports compliance with related articles in the UNCRC. Children's rights principles have also informed the drafting of other pieces of legislation such as the Health and Social Care (Community Health and Standards) Act 2003, the Regulation of Care (Scotland) Act 2001 and the National Care Standards in each part of the UK.

A shared responsibility

It is important to recognise that the responsibility for realisation of the rights of the child is a shared responsibility. Although the state has the primary responsibility according to the UNCRC, an equally important task rests upon staff in agencies (as the duty bearers for the state), parents or carers, and the wider community. There is a growing awareness and respect for the concept of human rights and this is increasingly evident in the development of policies and procedures in relation to children and young people. The rights agenda is perhaps nowhere more important, or more challenging, than with children placed in residential care.

Although the UK became a signatory to the UNCRC in 1991, there is still a lack of basic information about children's rights in some areas. This lack of understanding about the issue of children's rights contributes to a degree of confusion and suspicion in some institutional and practice settings. Based on a study of staff attitudes in residential care, Heron & Chakrabarti (2003) argue that 'the superficiality of the rights agenda has added to the complexities and tensions permeating residential provision' (2003: 356) and has also undermined practitioner morale in the process. A rights-based approach to any field of practice with children should not undermine morale, but achieving an optimal outcome does require the development of confident and assertive staff who can uphold children's rights while providing care, and setting rules and boundaries for young people.

The UNCRC provides a framework within which collaboration with the child can be encouraged and has a number of passages that speak specifically and clearly to care providers in order to ensure that the right to participation and involvement remains paramount. Some of the important articles in this regard will now be explored.

Activity

Look at the abbreviated copy of the UNCRC below:

1 Which of the articles speak about the rights of children and young people to participation?
2 Do any of the articles say that children in care should be treated differently from children who are not in care?

The United Nations Convention on the Rights of the Child

Article 1: Everyone under 18 has all these rights.
Article 2: The child has the right to protection against discrimination. This means that nobody can treat them badly because of their race, sex or religion, language, have a disability or are rich or poor.
Article 3: All adults should always do what is best for children.
Article 4: The child has the right to have their rights made a reality by the government.
Article 5: Children have the right to be given guidance by their parents and family.

Article 6: Children have the right to life.

Article 7:.Children have the right to have a name and a nationality.

Article 8: Children have the right to an identity.

Article 9: Children have the right to live with their parents unless it is bad for them.

Article 10: If children and their parents are living in separate countries they have the right to get back together and live in the same place.

Article 11: Children should not be kidnapped.

Article 12: Children have the right to an opinion and for it to be listened to and taken seriously.

Article 13: Children have the right to find out things and say what they think, through making art, speaking and writing, unless it breaks the rights of others.

Article 14: Children have the right to think what they like and be whatever religion they want to be with their parent's guidance.

Article 15: Children have the right to be with friends and join or set up clubs unless this breaks the rights of others.

Article 16: Children have the right to a private life. For instance, they can keep a diary that other people cannot see.

Article 17: Children have the right to collect information from radios, newspapers, TV etc. from all round the world. They should also be protected from information that could harm them.

Article 18: Children have the right to be brought up by their parents if possible.

Article 19: Children have the right to be protected from being hurt or badly treated.

Article 20: Children have the right to special protection if they can't live with their parents.

Article 21: Children have the right to have the best care if they are adopted or living in care.

Article 22: Children have the right to special protection if they are a refugee.

Article 23: If children are disabled, either mentally or physically they have the right to special care and education to help them develop.

Article 24: Children have the right to the best health possible and to medical care and to information to help them stay well.

Article 25: Children have the right to have their living arrangements checked regularly if they are living away from home.

Article 26: Children have the right to help from the government if they are poor or in need.

Article 27: Children have the right to a good enough standard of living. This means food, clothes and a place to live.

Article 28: Children have the right to education.

Article 29: Children have the right to education which develops their personality and abilities as much as possible.

Article 30: If children are a minority group due to race, religion or language they have the right to enjoy/practise/use their own culture, religion, language.

Article 31: Children have the right to play and relax by doing things like sports, music and drama.
Article 32: Children have the right to protection from work that is bad for their health or education.
Article 33: Children have the right to be protected from dangerous drugs.
Article 34: Children have the right to be protected from sexual abuse.
Article 35: No one is allowed to kidnap or sell a child.
Article 36: Children have the right to protection from any other kind of exploitation.
Article 37: Children have the right not to be punished in a cruel or hurtful way.
Article 38: Children have the right to protection in times of war. If a child is under 15 they should never be in the army or take part in battle.
Article 39: Children have the right to help if they have been hurt, neglected or badly treated.
Article 40: Children have the right to help in defending themselves if accused of breaking the law.
Article 41: Children have the right to any rights in laws in their country or internationally that give them better rights than these.
Article 42: All adults and children should know about this convention. Children have a right to learn about their rights and adults should learn about them too.

The convention has 54 articles in total. Article 43–54 are about how governments and international organisations will work to give children their rights.

Commentary on Activity

This table is taken from a children's rights training pack developed for the Scottish Institute for Residential Child Care by Stevens, Paterson and Vrouwenfelder (2004). The full text of the UNCRC is available on www. unicef.org. This commentary makes reference to the full text document.

Article 42 suggests that awareness of the UNCRC's main principles and provisions will be made 'widely known' through 'appropriate and active means to adults and children alike'.

Article 12 says that children and young people should be free to have opinions in all matters affecting them, and those views should be given due weight 'in accordance with the age and maturity of the child'. The underlying idea is that children have the right to be heard and to have their views taken seriously, including in any judicial or administrative proceedings affecting them.

Article 13 states that children have the right to seek out information and express themselves in the best way for them, as long as this does not infringe the rights of others. Other articles have the principle of participation inherent within them and you may have picked out some of these.

The principle of participation should operate to help practitioners acknowledge the right of children to freely express their views, as long as this does not encroach upon the rights of others. Residential workers and social workers need to bear in mind that children and young people are themselves important sources of information about their lives and what constitutes their 'best interests'. While *participation* is also a central concern in all discussions about children's rights, this principle cannot be practised in isolation or without a holistic appreciation of these other fundamental children's rights principles.

Article 20 says that any young person 'temporarily deprived of his or her family environment, or in whose best interests cannot be allowed to remain in that environment, shall be entitled to special protection', and particular regard for the 'ethnic, religious, cultural and linguistic background' shall play a role in decision-making and case management. Furthermore, **Article 25** suggests that authorities 'recognise the right of a child who has been placed by competent authorities for the purposes of care, protection or treatment ... to a periodic review of the treatment provided and all other circumstances relevant to his or her placement'. These reviews provide opportunities to actively engage a child as well as parents, family members or care providers, and educational and other concerned professionals. In other words, children and young people in residential care have a right to be treated differently from children who are not in care, insofar as they are entitled to special protection and reviews of their care.

The ethics of collaborative practice with children in residential care

While issues regarding capacity to participate should be considered with every person, the cognitive abilities of children and the power differentials between adults and children require special consideration. Both the British Association of Social Workers (BASW) Code of Ethics and the Code of Practice for Social Service Workers talk about promoting the rights of individuals. However, children are not mentioned specifically in the Code of Practice. In the BASW Code of Ethics, children are only specifically mentioned when it comes to a social worker's duty to protect vulnerable clients from harm. Once again, the child is cast in the role of potential victim, or as a dependent within this discourse. The child as active agent is not apparent.

Kroll (1995) points out that good collaboration with children starts with acknowledging the power differential between adults and children. She suggests that key issues arise in how adult professionals talk to children, how they clear their minds sufficiently to pay proper attention to them, and how they make genuine empathic contact. She argues strongly that practitioners working with children need a child-centred philosophy in order to engage meaningfully with them and that they need to *be* rather than *do*. 'Being' is where the practitioner spends time with the child simply for the sake of being with the child. Residential child care workers have the greatest opportunity for 'being', through the day-to-day experience of working with children in the lifespace of the unit. Social workers face a challenge in this area as they do not have so many readily available opportunities and therefore have to work imaginatively to create these. Because of this, there may be a chance that social workers will fall into the trap of 'doing'. An example of this might be making an appointment to see the child to go over their social work report for their care-plan review meeting. The timing, and the amount of time taken, is sometimes driven by the needs of the social worker rather than the child's needs at that moment.

Morrow & Richards (1996) in their discussion on the participation of children in research came to the conclusion that in everyday life, adults do not typically respect children's views and opinions. They believe that this increases the challenge of developing child-friendly approaches to involving children in research, in a way that is fair and respectful to them. The same could be said about the participation of children in their care and in the decision-making processes surrounding that activity. Sinclair and Gibbs (1998) in their study of 48 children's homes in England paint a disheartening picture of the level of participation of young people in their placement. Many of the children had no idea how long they would be in the children's home, or where their social worker thought they might go in the future. The researchers discovered that where care-plans were in place, the young people were to some extent mistaken about what the care-plan contained, most commonly when the social worker's plan did not match the young person's wishes. While, of course, it is not always possible to give each child what they may want in relation to their family having broken down, it is surely reasonable to expect that social workers and residential workers explain the plan of care to the child in language they can understand.

Thomas and O'Kane (1999) when studying looked-after children's participation in their care planning asked children to rank particular statements in order of importance. The children in the study ranked 'to have my say' and 'to be listened to' above 'to get what I want' when asked about the review process. From this it is clear that what children desire is a dialogue about what is happening to them, and a sense of involvement in their own care.

Activity

We have outlined how important it is to achieve the real participation of children in care. Yet, professionals must keep in mind the difficulties some children might face with participation. For example, the use of professional shorthand or jargon by adults, or the physical environment can have detrimental effects on participation. Give one example of how you would facilitate active and informed participation of looked-after children and young people in decisions that affect them:

1   at the day-to-day level of the residential unit
2   at child care reviews.

How to establish a culture of respect for children's rights in residential care

Adopting a thorough-going rights-based approach to practice is not likely to be any easier than any other approach which have tended to be needs-based. The complexities of practice may well increase but if practitioners know the UNCRC, are committed to its ideas, and are trained in how to apply it in practice, they will be equipped to proceed ethically with the daily challenges that face them. Establishing a culture of respect for children's rights also potentially provides a shared framework for inter-professional work with children. Implementing a rights-based approach requires initial and ongoing training for field social workers and residential child care workers in basic knowledge of what the UNCRC says and its application to children in care. Basic written and video resources should be provided for all practitioners, new residents and their family and carers based upon the core principle of participation.

Complaints procedures

Effective internal and external complaints procedures for all children and staff should be developed and promoted in a relevant way. The right to make complaints is enshrined in the regulations such as the National Minimum Care Standard for children's homes. Schedule 1, part 23, of the regulations state that children's homes 'must have arrangements for dealing with complaints' (Department of Health, 2002: 22). This type of legislative power under the regulations will ensure accountability and prevent workers from simply paying lip service to children's rights. Regular visits by social workers to residential units and ongoing communication with and accountability to external quality assurance representatives including Care Commission officers (Inspectors) are also an important factor. The establishment of an appropriate culture of children's rights requires that rights be seen within a wider context of human rights and adult relationships. This should include how residential workers treat each other, how social workers and residential workers relate to each other, and how the agency treats its staff as a whole. It is difficult for practitioners to adopt an empowering and rights-based approach to the children and young people in their care if they themselves do not feel that their rights are being respected.

Fostering this type of culture in a residential unit requires practical everyday actions by residential workers. Rights-based practice can be demonstrated by offering choice in matters such as décor, meal planning and choice of recreational activities; and if a young person's choices cannot be met in a specific situation it is important to explain why this is so. The creation of a culture of collaboration can also be promoted by making sure that children are given real opportunities to make their views known to the staff involved in their care. For example, if review or planning meetings are coming up, an adequate amount of time should be spent with the young person in helping them to develop their input for the meeting, as we explore below in more detail. While it is important that children and young people have access to independent advocacy services, it may be that the child needs the residential worker or the social worker to act as an advocate on their behalf at planning meetings. If either of these workers takes on this role, it should be negotiated with the child and supported by management. The child should be encouraged to record their views so that these can be rehearsed before meetings, or presented by the social worker or the residential worker if the child does not have the confidence or ability to speak within a group. There are many other examples that can be used, but the central point is that the residential workers and social workers should place the promotion of children's rights at the centre of the decision-making activity, rather than as an 'add-on'.

In the case of disabled children, their right to participate usually requires considerable advance planning and communication skills on the part of practitioners. Where there are parents involved, the reality of working with disabled children means that residential workers and social workers have to be very clear about who they are working with, and whose views they are taking into account. While the main focus of practice may be the child, all practitioners are required to maximise the involvement of parents in the care of their children and this can lead to challenges for the worker. The reality is that the parents of disabled children are used to fighting for their child, given the paucity of services available. For example, Stalker, Cadogan, Petrie, Jones and Murray (1999) reported that:

> families had to be desperate before they would get support. One mother said she 'has to kick up a fuss' to get anywhere: she had 'to threaten that she was on the point of having a breakdown'. (1999: 29)

As a result, parents may believe that they know what is best for their child without having gone through any process of participation with them. Hence, it is very important to ensure that what is being proposed on behalf of a disabled child reflects their best interests and that the social worker and the residential worker have gone through a process of trying to ascertain the child's views.

Participation-centred care practice

Children enter residential care because they have experienced a number of very
severe problems. As a result, their relationships with family and friends, or individuals in positions of authority, may have been very difficult and/or limited. Developing
meaningful relationships with such children can be extremely demanding, but it can
be made more satisfactory for both practitioner and child if participation is put at
the centre.

Participation between the child and the residential worker is the basis for any
change that occurs between them. However, positive change can only take place
between the child and worker if certain essential attributes are present. Thomas and
O'Kane (1999) identify several essential elements which need to be present in order
for children to feel more involved in their own care-planning:

- concern for others
- relationship
- genuineness
- creating the child's agenda
- choice, information and preparation
- time and activities.

In the following section we suggest how these elements can inform collaboration
with children.

Concern for others means that the residential worker sincerely cares about the child,
and that they accept the necessary responsibilities in dealing with the difficulties that
the child is experiencing.

Relationship refers to the involvement and investment which the residential worker
or social worker brings to the relationship with the child. These factors allow the
child to develop trust in the worker. This should include elements of support and
encouragement to the child or young person. The purpose of the child–worker relationship must also be taken into account when working directly with children and young
people. *Purpose* is a special element because, when it is consciously and deliberately

determined and communicated within the ethical base of residential care, it will make the relationship between the child and the residential worker unique from other kinds of relationships. The relationship should not be driven by a desire to be friendly or non-conflictual, because as Keith-Lucas states:

> The attempt to keep the relationship on a pleasant level is one of the greatest sources of ineffectual helping known to man ... But a relationship will grow wherever one person demonstrates to another both by his actions and his words that he respects the other, that he has concern for him and cares what happens to him, and that he is willing to both listen and to act helpfully. (1994: 48–9)

Therefore, although the relationship between the child and the residential worker share similar features with other kinds of relationships, there are fundamental differences. The essential features of the child's relationship with social workers and with residential workers are that they are a medium for change, they are driven by a purpose and above all they are participatory.

Active listening is the practitioner's ability to demonstrate that they understand the child's feelings and experiences. By entering the child's 'world' practitioners can begin to help establish cooperation and build the basis for collaboration.

Genuineness demands that the practitioner be open and honest with the child; that is, the worker should be trying to help because they want to, not because they are instructed to do so.

Creating the child's agenda acknowledges that although authority and power ultimately reside with staff, as they are the adults, it is important that the agenda comes from the child's needs, not what the adults in the situation want.

Choice, information and preparation requires the child to have an understanding of what the staff member is striving to achieve with them. This demands a degree of mutuality. Unless the child has a sense of why interventions are happening and their ability to have some control, the child can very easily feel disengaged from the process.

Time and activities are important. The children in the study valued time that was spent with them. They did not like the feeling that they had to have appointments, and they most valued just being with the worker when the need arose. Allied to this is *how* time is spent with children. Activities which help the child to communicate and make sense of the issues in their lives were seen to be the best way of spending time with them. This is helpful to keep in mind when one considers the potential for time to be spent with children by residential child care workers.

Activity
An 11-year-old child has been received into a residential unit as an emergency admission, due to a history of parental neglect.
Identify some of the differences that might exist between the worker's viewpoint about the problem or the family, and that of the child.

What young people in care tell us about collaboration

Several research studies and investigations use the voices and experiences of children and young people to report on their own realities. The work by Thomas and O'Kane cited above used quotes from young people to describe how they experienced their participation in planning and review meetings. The Who Cares? Scotland report called *Let's Face It* (Paterson et al., 2003) sought the views of young people about their whole experience of residential care. One of the key themes identified by the young people concerned involvement and participation in decision-making. The views expressed by the young people echoed the findings of Thomas and O'Kane. Young people valued it when they were listened to and their views promoted. Even when the decisions taken did not reflect their wishes, some form of acknowledgment that their views were taken into account was important. This degree of involvement also helped foster respect and trust in the staff who worked with them. Not surprisingly, if a young person's views were not taken into account, this served to alienate young people and caused fear, distress and anger.

Conclusion

Residential child care exists for children and young people. It should provide a positive and viable way of caring for them and meeting their needs. However, it is important that all professionals working with children have a good knowledge of children's rights. The involvement of children in decisions affecting their life should be real and not tokenistic. Workers need to be self-aware and ensure that some of the prevailing attitudes about childhood do not undermine their own ability to take a rights-based, child-centred approach. A child-centred approach should never just mean considering the best interests of the child from the perspective of the carer; it must also consider what the child thinks is best for themselves. Above all the child should be listened to and respected as a partner in their own care and collaboration with the child should form the basis of all work.

Further Reading

Foley, P., Roche, J. & Tucker, S. (2001). *Children in society*. Basingstoke: Palgrave.
This is an excellent general overview of the role and place of children in society. It helps the reader to understand some of the social constructions around childhood, and also gives a good introduction to the area of childhood studies.

Emond, R. (2003). Putting the care into residential care: the role of young people. *Journal of Social Work, 3*(3), 321–37.
This article shows the positive nature of support by young people for young people in care, and gives a strong argument for increasing the participation of children in care.

Conclusion: Children Tell It Like It Is

The legendary singer – and young person – Eddie Cochran once wrote a song about some of the difficulties of being young. In his song, *Summertime Blues,* he sang with great feeling about how young people can be almost invisible in the eyes of the powerful ('I'd like to help you son but you're too young to vote').

The sentiments expressed by Eddie Cochran had a strong resonance with young people when *Summertime Blues* was a hit in 1958. Some things have changed since then. Children now have a voice at the United Nations, and Western society is becoming more aware of children's rights. However, the question of whether children are really listened to is another matter. The sense of powerlessness expressed in the song can still be real for many children and young people. Therefore it is important that the voices of children are heard at this point, as we summarise some of our findings about collaboration.

In this concluding chapter, some of the key themes of the earlier text are revisited. The chapter addresses some of the main messages which should be kept in mind for collaborative practice, illustrates the points with the voices of children and young people in care, and suggests some key practice questions for each area. The sections in this chapter are illustrated with the experiences and opinions of children and young people in residential care (Paterson et al., 2003; Voice of the Child in Care (VCC), 2004; and Ward, Skuse & Munro, 2005). As we have argued, this is because there is much to be learned from actually listening to children in care. They are experiencing this type of care every day and are best placed to give residential workers and social workers some clues as to how to advance their collaborative practice.

Understanding policy and contexts

> My social worker seemed to wait to find me the perfect placement, so I kept on moving and moving – all over the country. (VCC, 2004: 23)

The use of residential child care, like any other area of social policy, is affected by a range of factors such as the prevailing ideology of those in power, public pressure and opinion, its own history, and the legislation and guidance that defines it. Residential child care has a long history and has had to develop in the context of a society which almost invariably constructs the service in a negative and ultimately unhelpful way. Perhaps the most pervasive perception at the moment is the notion of residential child care as a place of last resort. However, this perception can lead to an unduly pessimistic view which overlooks the positive experiences that children can have as illustrated by findings such as Ward et al. (2005). While we would not want to deny that some residential units have been found to offer a poor quality of care, or that there are widespread failings in the educational provision for looked-after children, it is important that any criticism of the service is not over-generalised. Residential workers and social workers should have an understanding of where residential child care came from and how it continues to meet the needs of some of the most vulnerable children in our society. They also have an obligation to keep up-to-date with policy changes, to ensure that their practice reflects contemporary trends.

Key practice questions on policy are:

- What are the current policies, guidance and legislation that govern residential child care?
- How are those policies, guidance and legislation made real at my own local level?
- How do I keep up to date with changes in policy, guidance and legislation?
- How are my potential partners in collaborative practice affected by policy and legislative changes?

Understanding care

> Care is to make sure that the person is well looked after – until they can take care of themselves. (VCC, 2004: 14)

Collaborative practice in residential child care is about ensuring the best possible outcomes for a child. However, it is also about ensuring that the child experiences being cared for in the process. Care as an activity has in many ways been undervalued in our society, yet it is care-giving which has the most profound impact on a child's development and their subsequent life outcomes. However, the notion of care is not easy to define. It differs in significant ways for each of the professional groups discussed in the book. These differences can lead to unnecessary tensions between potential collaborative partners if they are not clearly understood. It has been argued in this book that social workers and residential workers have different but complementary roles to play in this process. Both of these groups of workers should endeavour to understand and analyse each other's understandings of care. More importantly, each should be alert to the dangers of professional conflict that may be a by-product of differences in status and focus of work. We should respect and value the other's approach to care in order to promote collaborative practice.

Key practice questions on understanding care are:

- What philosophies and codes of practice underpin my understanding of care?
- How might these differ from other professionals involved with children in residential child care?
- How do I make these understandings explicit to others with whom I will be collaborating?

Understanding organisations

> Often the big things that are going on, you are left in the dark. For example, *Me:* 'When can I go home?' *Social Worker:* 'When a risk assessment is completed.' I don't even know what a risk assessment is! (VCC, 2004: 53)

All of the professionals mentioned in the book are located within larger agencies and organisations. Understanding how organisations work and the effects that they can have on collaborative practice helps to enhance this process. Children themselves will pick up very quickly if someone is being driven by organisational imperatives or whether they are truly interested in them, as illustrated in the quote above. In the same way, the professionals who have a key role to play in the lives of children in care should also become more self-aware of the organisational imperatives which drive both them and their counterparts in other agencies. It is also important to understand what professionalism means in practice, and how important their professional identity is to the various practitioners we have examined in this book.

Key practice questions about organisations are:

- What do I know about the organisations for whom my collaborative partners work?
- Are those organisations going through changes and how might this impact on my work with them?
- What resource implications are around in the different organisations that I should be aware of?

Understanding partnership with parents

> Honestly, I don't think my social worker has seen my parents or other members of my family in the past year and a half as a visit. He's seen my mother 2 or 3 times at meetings but that's about it. (Paterson et al., 2003: 57)

Family is one of the most important influences on the lives of all children. For children in residential care, family has the same significance, although it may be the locus of much distress and trauma. Social workers who are based in the community tend to be more familiar with working with families in general, and with parents in particular. However, residential workers have a primary responsibility for the child and may not be so skilled in this area, therefore it is a challenge to them to ensure that they work in partnership with parents. Increasingly, residential staff are undertaking outreach and family work with parents. Children will grow up to be adults and will not be 'looked-after' indefinitely. Many make the choice to return to their parents and it is therefore incumbent on social workers and residential workers to ensure that positive links are maintained. In most cases, parents of children in care still have most of their rights and responsibilities in relation to their children. Whilst helping young people with trauma and loss, these rights and responsibilities should be kept in mind by social workers and residential workers alike.

Key practice questions about working with parents are:

- How much do I know about the family of the child in care, in its widest sense?
- Am I welcoming to the parent or parents of the child?
- What do I really feel about this parent and how can I make sure that my feelings do not get in the way of partnership?
- What does the child want in relation to their parents?

Understanding collaboration with children

> If we don't like something, they could come to an agreement with us and give us something instead of what we don't want. Don't just tell us, ask our opinion and explain what's going on. (Paterson et al., 2003: 21)

The UNCRC has placed children's rights firmly on the agenda for all professionals who work with children in any setting. However, the need for the UNCRC as an explicit statement outlining children's rights arose because many children were not having their basic rights met. Children in residential care have experienced many problems and are at risk of many kinds of social exclusion (Kendrick, 2005). It is the duty of every professional who works with them to ensure that their rights are upheld. In particular, the UNCRC talks about children's rights to participate in decisions about their own lives. Children in residential care are in a situation where their lives are highly scrutinised and recorded, and many aspects of their life are taken over by the state. However, the state still has a duty to ensure that participation happens. Residential workers and social workers are in the best position to promote this set of rights. They are the key duty bearers in ensuring that the voices of children are heard in any decisions made about them. They should make collaboration with children into a real and meaningful process. This in turn provides a good role model for children and makes them feel valued.

Key practice questions for working with children are:

- Do I know the UNCRC?
- How do I implement a rights-based approach in my work with children and young people?
- When I talk to children, am I really listening to what they want, and not imposing my own values on this?
- Do I need extra help or training to assist me to communicate with children and young people?

Understanding the importance of education and health care

> You know some people in their lives go through a bad time and now is maybe my time. You don't really know what's wrong with you. I feel like I'm in this dark dimension and I can't find the light. It's like I've got problems with school, problems with friends and I'm trying to be good at school, and it's working but then just at the wrong time, the wrong place, I do something and I get into trouble for it. (Paterson et al., 2003: 37)

Apart from residential workers and social workers, we identified teachers and nurses as two of the most important professionals involved in the lives of children. This is not to belittle the work done by other professionals. However, health and education play such an important part in the life outcomes of children that we felt that we had to give some degree of priority to this area. Teachers and nurses occupy their own professional space, and have a long-established and widely respected role in our society. They have distinct approaches, definitions and identities when it comes to providing their services to children. It is important for residential workers and social workers to understand where these differences lie and how they can be viewed in a positive manner, and not as barriers to collaborative practice. By striving to understand how nurses and teachers view their role, and by supporting them in dealing with children who may be uncomfortable or alienated at school, then collaboration has a chance of being much more successful.

Key practice questions in health and education are:

- How do nurses and teachers view their role in relation to children in residential care?
- What do their codes of practice say in relation to their approach to collaboration?
- What barriers to collaboration might exist in the structures surrounding health care and educational provision?
- How important do I think health care and educational provision are to children in residential care?

The importance of collaborative practice in social work and social care education

Collaboration is a necessary component of professional social work practice. As we noted in the introduction, this is explicitly recognised in the competences laid down in the Subject Benchmark Statement for Social Work by the Quality Assurance Agency for Higher Education (2000). Collaborative practice is represented in each of the five core areas of knowledge and understanding in the Benchmark Statement, which states that social workers must understand and be able to apply and evaluate the following:

- the relationship between policies, law and professional boundaries in shaping the nature of services provided in inter-disciplinary contexts, working across professional boundaries and within different disciplinary groups
- the significance of inter-relationships with other social services, especially education, housing, health, income maintenance and criminal justice
- the links and potential conflicts between the codes defining ethical practice held by different professional groups
- approaches and methods of intervention in a range of settings including group care
- the factors and processes that facilitate effective inter-disciplinary, inter-agency and inter-professional collaboration and partnership.

One of the aims of this book has been to outline some of the issues which are of relevance to this important area of social work education, and provide some opportunities to reflect on this. By paying attention to the need for collaborative practice at the earliest stage of professional development, there is a real opportunity for social workers and residential workers to make a genuine difference to the lives of children in care.

The final word

Hopefully, the book will have provided some food for thought for practitioners working with children in residential care. Collaborative practice is of major importance in ensuring that the lives of children in care are as enriched as possible. Perhaps it would be best to leave the final words to the young people themselves so that we remember why we are involved in their lives:

> The staff were good ... they were friendly and had excellent attitudes towards you. They were just there for you. (Ward et al., 2005: 14)

Further Reading

Paterson, S., Watson, D. & Whiteford, J. (2003). *Let's face it: young people in care tell it as it is.* Glasgow: Who Cares? Scotland.
This report was produced by Who Cares? Scotland, which is the main advocacy group for children in care in Scotland. The report sought to outline the most important issues for young people who are looked after and accommodated, and to develop a set of recommendations for practice based on their views. The report, based on a 14-month consultation with 90 young people, is largely written using the voice and opinions of young people.

Ward, H., Skuse, T. & Munro. E. (2005). The best of times, the worst of times: young people's views of care and accommodation. *Adoption and Fostering, 29*(1), 8–17.
This study looked at a cohort of 242 children who had experienced at least one year of being looked after, across six local authorities in England. The paper explored what children did and did not like about being looked after. The paper contained largely positive responses from the children, and once again used direct quotes from children to emphasise points.

Voice of the Child in Care (2004). *Start with the child, stay with the child.* London: NCB.
This report is based on the views of children and young people, and has been written to provide a very user-friendly guide for professionals, managers and policy-makers about what is important to children and young people in relation to their care experiences.

References

Ainsworth, F. (1997). *Family-centred group care: model building.* Aldershot: Ashgate.

Ainsworth. F. & Fulcher, L. (1985). *Group care for children: concept and issues.* London: Tavistock.

Alter, C. (2000). Interorganisational collaboration in the task environment. In R. Patti, *The handbook of social welfare management.* London: Sage.

Anglin, J. (1999). The uniqueness of child and youth care: a personal perspective. *Child and Youth Care Forum, 28*(2), 143–150.

Arcellus, J., Bellerby, T. & Vostanis, P. (1999). A mental health service for young people in the care of the local authority. *Clinical Child Psychology and Psychiatry, 4*(2), 233–245.

Aries, P. (1962). *Centuries of childhood.* Harmondsworth: Penguin.

Barry, M. (2001). *A sense of purpose: care leavers' view of growing up.* Edinburgh: Save the Children.

Barton, C. (2003). Allies and enemies: the service user as care coordinator. In J. Weinstein, C. Whittington and T. Leiba (Eds.), *Collaboration in social work practice.* London: Jessica Kingsley Publishers.

Becker, H. (1963). *Outsiders: studies in the sociology of deviance.* New York: The Free Press.

(The) Beckford Report (1985). *A child in trust: the report of the panel inquiry into the circumstances surrounding the death of Jasmine Beckford.* London Borough of Brent.

Berger, P. & Luckman, T. (1967). *The social construction of reality: a treatise in the sociology of knowledge.* New York: Doubleday.

Berridge, D. & Brodie, I. (1998). *Children's homes revisited.* London: Jessica Kingsley Publishers.

Berridge, D. & Cleaver, H. (1987). *Foster home breakdown.* Oxford: Blackwell.

Biehal, N., Clayden, J., Stein, M. & Wade, J. (1995). *Moving on: young people and leaving care schemes.* London: HMSO.

Biggs, S. (2003). Interprofessional collaboration: problems and prospects. In J. Ovretviet, P. Matthias and T. Thomson, *Interprofessional working in health and social care.* London: Macmillan.

Bilson, A. & Barker, R. (1995). Parental contact with children fostered and in residential care after the Children Act 1989. *British Journal of Social Work, 25*(3), 367–381.

Booth, T. (1983). Collaboration and the social division of planning. In J. Lishman (Ed.), *Research Highlights No. 7: Collaboration and conflict: working with others.* Aberdeen: University of Aberdeen.

Bottery, M. (1998). *Professionals and policy: management strategy in a competitive world.* London: Cassell.

Bowlby, J. (1982). *Attachment and loss: Vol. 1. Attachment.* New York: Basic Books. (Originally published 1969).

Boyce, P. (2002). *A different class? Educational attainment – the views and experiences of looked after young people.* Glasgow: Who Cares? Scotland.

Brannen, J. & O'Brien, M. (Eds). (1995). *Children in families: research and policy.* London: Falmer Press.

Brolinson, P.G., Price, J.H. & Ditmyer, M. (2001). Nurses' perceptions of complementary and alternative medical therapies. *Journal of Community Health, 26*(3), 175–189.

Brooks, I. (2002). *Organisational Behaviour: individuals, groups and organisation.* London: Prentice Hall.

Bryce, G. (2004). *The health of looked after children and young people: Conference report.* Edinburgh: NHS Health Scotland.

Bullock, R., Little, M. & Millham, S. (1993). *Going home.* Aldershot: Dartmouth.

Butler, I. & Drakeford, M. (2005). *Scandal, social policy and social welfare* (revised 2nd ed.). Bristol: BASW/Policy Press.

Butler, I. & Payne, H. (1997). The health of children looked after by the local authority. *Adoption & Fostering, 21*(2), 28–35.

Cambridge Dictionary Online. http://dictionary.cambridge.org/

(The) Carlile Report (1987). *A child in mind: the protection of children in a responsible society: The report of the commission of inquiry into the circumstances surrounding the death of Kimberly Carlile.* London Borough of Greenwich.

Central Council for Education and Training in Social Work (CCETSW) (1992). *Residential child care in the Diploma in Social Work.* London: CCETSW.

Challis, L. (1988). *Joint approaches to social policy: rationality and practice.* Cambridge: Cambridge University Press.

Clark, C. (2000). *Social work ethics: politics, principles and practice.* Basingstoke: Palgrave.

Cleveland Report (1988). *Report of the inquiry into child abuse in Cleveland 1987.* London: HMSO.

Cliffe, D. with Berridge, D. (1991). *Closing children's homes – an end to residential care?* London: NCB.

(The) Climbié Report (2003). *Report of an inquiry by Lord Laming.* London: HMSO.

Clyde Report (1992). *Report of the inquiry into the removal of children from Orkney in February 1991.* Edinburgh: HMSO.

Coffey, M., Dugdill. L. & Tattersall, A. (2004). Stress in social services: mental well-being, constraints and job satisfaction. *British Journal of Social Work, 34*, 735–746.

(The) Colwell Report (1974). *Report of the committee of inquiry into the care and supervision provided in relation to Maria Colwell.* London: HMSO.

Compton, B. & Galaway, B. (1999). *Social work processes* (6th ed.). Pacific Grove, CA: Brooks/Cole Publishing.

Crimmens, D. & Milligan, I. (2005). Residential child care: becoming a positive choice? In D. Crimmens and I. Milligan (Eds.), *Facing forward: residential child care in the 21st century.* Lyme Regis: Russell House Publishing.

Department for Education and Skills (2003) *Every child matters,* CM 5860, London: The Stationery Office.

Department for Education and Skills/Department of Health (2000). *Guidance on the education of young people in public care.* London: HMSO.

Department of Health (1998). *Caring for children away from home: messages from research.* London: Department of Health/Wiley.

Department of Health (2000). *Promoting the health of looked after children.* London: Department of Health/Quality Protects.

Department of Health (2002). *National minimum standard: children's homes regulations.* London: HMSO.

Department of Health (2003). *Learning for collaborative practice*. London: Department of Health.

Department of Health/Quality Protects (1999). *The government's objectives for children's social services*. London: Department of Health/Quality Protects.

Dixon, J. & Stein, M. (2002). *Still a bairn? Throughcare and aftercare services in Scotland: final report to the Scottish Executive*. York: University of York.

Dyer, W. (1985). The cycle of cultural evolution in organisations. In R. Kilmann et al. (Eds.), *Gaining control of the corporate culture*. San Francisco: Jossey-Bass.

Easen, P., Atkins, M. & Dyson, A. (2000). Inter-professional collaboration and conceptualisations of practice. *Children and Society, 14*, 355–367.

Emond, R. (2003). Putting the care into residential care: the role of young people. *Journal of Social Work, 3*(3), 321–337.

Erikson, E. (1959). Identity and the life cycle. *Psychological Issues, 1*, 1–7.

Fallona, C. (2001). *Pre-service teachers' perception of manner in teaching*. New York: Teacher's College Press.

Ferguson, H. & O'Reilly, M. (2001). *Keeping children safe*. Dublin: Farmar.

Foley, P., Roche, J. & Tucker. S. (2001). *Children in society*. Basingstoke: Palgrave.

Frost, N. & Stein, M. (1989). *The politics of child welfare*. Hemel Hempstead: Harvester Wheatsheaf.

Fulcher, L. (2001). Differential assessment of residential group care for children and young people. *British Journal of Social Work, 31*, 417–435.

Gallagher, B., Brannan, C., Jones, R. & Westwood, S. (2004). Good practice in the education of children in public care. *British Journal of Social Work, 34*, 1133–60.

Garnet, L. (1995). *The educational attainments and destinations of young people looked after by Humberside County Council*. Hull: Departments of Education and Social Services, Humberside County Council.

Gascoigne, E. (1995). *Working with parents as partners in SEN*. London: David Fulton.

Gaskell, M. (1965). The residential worker. In *Change and the child in care*, the Annual Review of the Residential Child Care Association. London: RCA.

Gastmans, C., Dierckx, B. & Schotsmans, P. (1998). Nursing considered as moral practice: a philosophical-ethical interpretation of nursing. *Kennedy Institute of Ethics Journal, 8*(1), 43–69.

General Social Care Council (2002). *Code of practice for social care workers*. London: GSCC.

General Teaching Council for England (2004). *Statement of professional values and practice for teachers*. Retrieved January 12, 2005, from www.gtce.org.uk/gtcinfo/code.asp

General Teaching Council for Scotland (2004). *Professionalism in practice*. Edinburgh: GTC for Scotland.

Gilligan, C. (1982). *In a different voice*. Boston: Harvard University Press.

Goffman E. (1961). *Asylums. Essays on the social situation of mental patients and other inmates*. New York: Doubleday.

Gottesman, M. (Ed.) (1991). *Residential child care: an international handbook*. London: Whiting & Birch/SCA.

Hallett, C. & Birchall, E. (1992). *Coordination and child protection: a review of the literature*. London: HMSO.

Haralambos, M. (2000). *Sociology: themes and perspectives* (5th ed.) London: Collins.

Hawthorn, M. (2005). Overcoming the barriers. In D. Crimmens and I. Milligan (Eds.), *Facing forward: residential child care in the 21st century*. Lyme Regis: Russell House.

Hendrick, H. (2003). *Child welfare: historical dimensions, contemporary debate.* Bristol: The Policy Press.

(The) Henry Report (1987). *Whose child? The report of the public inquiry into the death of Tyra Henry.* London Borough of Lambeth.

Heron, G. & Chakrabarti, M. (2003). Exploring the perceptions of staff towards children and young people living in community-based children's homes. *Journal of Social Work, 3*(1), 81–98.

Hill, M. (2000). Inclusiveness in residential child care. In M. Chakrabarti and M. Hill (Eds.), *Residential child care: international perspectives on links with families.* London: Jessica Kingsley.

HMI & SWSI (2001). *Learning with care: the education of children looked after away from home by local authorities.* Report of a joint inspection undertaken by HM Inspectors of Schools and the Social Work Services Inspectorate. Edinburgh: Scottish Executive.

Holman, B. (1995). *The evacuation: a very British revolution.* Oxford: Lion Publishing.

Holman, B. (1996). *The corporate parent: Manchester children's department 1948–71.* London: NISW.

Holman, B. (2001). *Champions for children: the lives of modern child care pioneers.* Bristol: The Policy Press.

Home Office, Ministry of Health and Ministry of Education (1946). *The report of the care of children committee* (Curtis Report). London: HMSO.

Hopson, B. & Adams, J. (1976). Towards an understanding: defining some boundaries of transition dynamics. In J. Adams, J. Hayes and B. Hopson (Eds.), *Transition: understanding and managing personal change.* London: Martin Robertson.

House of Commons (1998). *Report of the Select Committee on Health into the services for children looked after by local authorities.* London: The Stationery Office.

Jack, R. (Ed.) (1999). *Residential versus community care: the role of institutions in welfare provision.* Basingstoke: Macmillan.

Jackson, S. & Sachdev, D. (2001). *Better education, better futures.* Ilford: Barnardo's.

James, A., Jenks, C. & Prout, A. (1998). *Theorising childhood.* Cambridge: Polity Press.

Jordan, B. (1997). Partnership with service users in child protection and family support. In N. Parton (Ed.), *Child protection and family support: tensions, contradictions and possibilities.* London: Macmillan.

Joseph, S. (Ed.) (1999). *A voice for the child: the inspirational words of Janusz Korczak.* Retrieved June 1, 2005, from www.korczak.org.uk/portfolio

Kahan, B. (1994). *Growing up in groups.* National Institute for Social Work, Research Unit. London: HMSO.

Kant, I. (1964). *Groundwork of the metaphysics of morals.* New York: Harper Row.

Karger, H.J. (1983). Science, research and social work: who controls the profession? *Social Work, 28*(3), 200–5.

Keith-Lucas, A. (1994). *Giving and taking help* (2nd Ed.). North Carolina: NAACSW.

Kelly, B. & Hill, M. (1994). *Working together to help children and families.* Glasgow: NCH Action for Children.

Kendrick, A. (2005). Social exclusion and social inclusion: themes and issues in residential child care. In D. Crimmens and I. Milligan (Eds.) *Facing forward: residential child care in the 21st century.* Lyme Regis: Russell House Publishing.

Kent, R. (1997). *Children's safeguards review.* Edinburgh: Social Work Services Inspectorate/ Scottish Office.

Kroll, B. (1995). Working with children. In T. Kaganas, M. King and C. Piper (Eds.), *Legislating for harmony: partnership and the Children Act 1989.* London: Jessica Kingsley.

Kurtz, Z. (2001). Service innovation: learning from the 24 projects. *Young Minds Magazine 54*, 1–3.

Laing, R.D. (1965). *The divided self – an existential study in sanity & madness.* London: Pelican Books.

Lempp, H. (1995). Has nursing lost its way? Nursing: no regrets. *British Medical Journal, 311*(7000), 307–308.

Levy, A. & Kahan, B. (1991). *The Pindown experience and the protection of children: The report of the Staffordshire Child Care Inquiry 1990.* Stafford: Staffordshire County Council.

Lewicki, R., Barry, B., Saunders, D. & Minton, J. (2003). *Essentials of negotiation.* New York: McGraw-Hill.

Lewin, R. (2001). *Complexity: life at the edge of chaos* (2nd Ed.). London: Phoenix.

Lewis, H. (2000). Children in public care: overcoming barriers to effective mental health. *Young Minds Magazine, 46*, 16–18.

Lindsay, M. (Ed.) (1997). *Learning to care: caring to learn.* Glasgow: Centre for Residential Child Care.

Lindstrom, M. & Seybold, P.B. (2004). *Brandchild.* London: Kogan Page.

McKay, M. (1980). Planning for permanent placement. *Adoption & Fostering, 4*(1), 19–21. Reprinted in M. Hill (2002). *Shaping childcare practice in Scotland: key papers on adoption and fostering.* London: BAAS.

Maclean, K. & Connelly, G. (2005). Still room for improvement: the educational experiences of looked after children in Scotland. In D. Crimmens and I. Milligan (Eds.), *Facing forward: residential child care in the 21st century.* Lyme Regis: Russell House.

Maier, H.W. (1981). Essential components in care and treatment environments for children. In F. Ainsworth and L. Fulcher (Eds.), *Group care for children: concepts and issues.* London: Tavistock.

McCann, J., James, A., Wilson, S. & Dunn, G. (1996). Prevalence of psychiatric disorders in young people in the care system. *British Medical Journal, 313*, 1529–1530.

Meagher, G. & Parton, N. (2004). Modernising social work and the ethics of care. *Social Work and Society, 2*(1), 10–27.

Meltzer, H., Lader, D., Corbin, T., Goodman, R. & Ford, T. (2004). *The mental health of young people looked after by local authorities in Scotland.* London: Office of National Statistics.

Milligan, I. (1998). Residential child care is not social work! *Social Work Education, 17*(3), 275–285.

Milligan, I. (2004). *LEAP Project: final evaluation report.* Glasgow: University of Strathclyde.

Milligan, I. (in press). Three Strong Women. *Scottish Journal of Residential Child Care.*

Milligan, I., Kendrick, A. & Avan, G. (2005). *'Nae too bad': a survey of staff morale and motivation in residential child care in Scotland.* Glasgow: Scottish Institute for Residential Child Care.

Morrow, V. & Richards, M. (1996). The ethics of social research with children: an overview. *Children and Society, 10*(2), 90–105.

(The) Ness Report (2003). *Report of the Caleb Ness inquiry.* Edinburgh: Lothian and Borders Child Protection Committee.

Noddings, N. (1996). The cared for. In N. Noddings, S. Gordon and P. Benner (Eds.), *Caregiving: readings in knowledge, practice, ethics and politics.* Pennsylvania: University of Pennsylvania Press.

Noddings, N., Gordon, S. & Benner, P. (Eds.) (1996). *Caregiving: readings in knowledge, practice, ethics and politics.* Pennsylvania: University of Pennsylvania Press.

Nursing and Midwifery Council (2004). *Code of professional conduct: standards for conduct, performance and ethics.* London: NMC.

Packman, J. (1993). From prevention to partnership: child welfare services across three decades. *Children & Society, 7*(2), 183–195.

Page, R. & Clark, G. (1977). *Who Cares? Young people in care speak out.* London: NCB.

Papernow, P. (Ed.) (1993). *Becoming a step-family: patterns of development in remarried families.* Boston: The Analytic Press.

Parsloe, P. (1981). *Social service area teams.* London: Allen and Unwin.

Parton, N. (1991). *Governing the family: child care, child protection and the state.* London: Macmillan.

Parton, N. (1998). Ideology, politics and policy. In O. Stevenson, *Child welfare in the UK.* Oxford: Blackwell Science.

Parton, N. (2004). From Maria Colwell to Victoria Climbié: reflections on public inquiries into child abuse a generation apart. *Child Abuse Review, 13*(2), 80–94.

Parton, N., Thorpe, D. & Wattam, C. (1997). *Child protection: risk and the moral order.* London: Macmillan.

Paterson, S., Watson, D. & Whiteford. J. (2003). *Let's face it: young people in care tell it as it is.* Glasgow: Who Cares? Scotland.

Payne, M. (1996). *What is professional social work?* Birmingham: Venture.

Peters, T. & Waterman, R. (1982). *In search of excellence.* New York: Harper Row.

Pilkington, K. (2006). *From rescue to partnership.* University of Strathclyde, PhD thesis.

Pollock, L. (1983). *Forgotten children: parent–child relations from 1500 to 1900.* Cambridge: Cambridge University Press.

Polnay, L. & Ward, H. (2000). Promoting the health of looked after children. *British Medical Journal, 320,* 661–662.

Prior, J. (2002). *A genealogy of social work: moral enquiry for education.* University of Strathclyde, PhD thesis.

Prior, J. (forthcoming). *The virtue ethics of Alistair Macintyre in the context of social care practice.*

Quality Assurance Agency (2000). *Subject benchmark statement for social work.* Gloucester: Quality Assurance Agency for Higher Education.

Quinn, P. (2000). *In from the edge.* Glasgow: Centre for Residential Child Care.

Reich, W. (Ed.) (1995). *Encyclopedia of bioethics.* New York: Simon and Schuster.

Residential Care Health Project (2004). *Forgotten children: addressing the health needs of looked after children and young people.* Edinburgh: NHS Lothian.

Roe, W. (2005). *21st century review: an interim report.* Edinburgh: Scottish Executive.

Rogers, C.R. (2003). *Client centred therapy.* New York: Constable and Robinson.

Rowe, J. & Lambert, L. (1973). *Children who wait.* London: Association of British Adoption Agencies.

Scott, T., Mannion, R., Davies, H. & Marshall, M. (2003). *Healthcare performance and organizational culture.* Oxford: Radcliffe.

Scott. J. & Hill, M. (2004). The looking after children and young people in Scotland materials. *Scottish Journal of Residential Child Care,* February/March 2004, 17–30.

Scottish Commission for the Regulation of Care (2004). *A review of the quality of care homes in Scotland in 2004.* Dundee: SCRC.

Scottish Executive (2001). *For Scotland's children.* Edinburgh: Scottish Executive.

Scottish Executive (2003a). *National care standards: care homes for children and young people.* Edinburgh: Scottish Executive.

Scottish Executive (2003b). *SQA examination results in Scottish schools 2002–03.* Edinburgh: Scottish Executive.

Scottish Executive (2004a). *Children looked after 2003–04.* Edinburgh: Scottish Executive National Statistics publication.

Scottish Executive (2004b). *Supporting young people leaving care in Scotland: regulations and guidance on services for young people ceasing to be looked after by local authorities: regulations and guidance.* Edinburgh: Scottish Executive.

Scottish Executive (June 2005). *Getting it right for every child: consultation.* Edinburgh: Scottish Executive. Retrieved July 24, 2005, from www.scotland.gov.uk/publications

Scottish Office, Social Work Services Group (1997). *The Children (Scotland) Act 1995: Regulations and Guidance, vol.2.* Edinburgh: Scottish Office/HMSO.

Sherif, M. (1967). *Group conflict and cooperation.* London: Routledge and Kegan Paul.

Short Committee (1984). *House of Commons Social Services Committee Report on children in care.* London: HMSO.

Sinclair, I. & Gibbs, I. (1998). *Children's homes: a study in diversity.* London: John Wiley and Sons.

Skinner, A. (1992). *Another kind of home: a review of residential child care.* Edinburgh: Scottish Office.

Smale, G. (1977). *Prophesy, behaviour and change: an examination of self-fulfilling prophesies in helping relationships.* London: Routledge and Kegan Paul.

Smale, G. (1998). *Managing change through innovation.* London: The Stationery Office.

Smith, M. (2003). Towards a professional identity and knowledge base: Is residential child care still social work? *Journal of Social Work, 3*(2), 235–252.

Smith, M. & Milligan, I. (2005). The expansion of secure education in Scotland: In the best interests of the child? *Youth Justice, 4*(3), 178–191.

Sockett, H. (1993). *The moral base for teacher professionalism.* New York: Teacher's College Press.

Stalker, K., Cadogan, L., Petrie, M., Jones, C. & Murray, J. (1999). *If you don't ask, you don't get. Review of services to people with learning disabilities: the views of people who use services and their carers.* Edinburgh: Central Research Unit.

Stevens, I. (2000). Family reconstitution and the implications for group care workers. In M. Chakrabarti and M. Hill (Eds.) *Residential child care: international perspectives on links with families and peers.* London: Jessica Kingsley.

Stevens, I., Paterson, S. & Vrouwenfelder, E. (2004). *Children's rights: promoting and implementing rights in residential care. A training pack.* Glasgow: University of Strathclyde, the Scottish Institute for Residential Child Care.

Strathclyde Regional Council (1978). *Room to grow: report of a special social work committee on child care in Strathclyde.* Glasgow: SRC.

Strathclyde Regional Council (1983). *Home or away? Residential child care strategy for the eighties.* Glasgow: SRC.

Thomas, N. & O'Kane, C. (1999). Children's participation in review and planning meetings when they are looked-after in middle childhood. *Child and Family Social Work, 4*(3), 221–230.

Thorpe, D., Paley, J., Smith, D. & Green, D. (1980). *Out of care: the community support of juvenile offenders.* London: Allen and Unwin.

Triseliotis, J. (1991). Perceptions of permanence. *Adoption & Fostering, 15*, 4.

Triseliotis, J., Borland, M. & Hill, M. (2000). *Delivering foster care.* London: BAAF.

Tronto, J. (1993). *Moral boundaries: a political argument for an ethic of care.* London: Routledge.

Turner, J. (1991). *Social influence.* Buckingham: Open University Press.

UNCRC (UN Committee on the Rights of the Child). (2002). *2nd concluding observations report on the UK.* Geneva: UNCRC.

Utting, W. (1991). *Children in the public care: a review of residential care.* London: DoH/HMSO.

Utting, W. (1997). *People like us: the report of the review of the safeguards for children living away from home.* London: Stationery Office.

van Beinum, M., Martin, A. & Bonnett, C. (2002). Catching children as they fall: mental health promotion in residential childcare in East Dunbartonshire. *Scottish Journal of Residential Child Care,* August/September, 14–22.

Vernelle, B. (1994). *Understanding and using groups.* London: Whiting and Birch.

Villiotti, D. (1995). Embracing the chaos: moving from child-centred to family-centred. *Residential Treatment for Children and Youth, 13*(2), 41–45.

Visher, J. & Visher, E. (1987). *Step-families: a guide to working with step-parents and step-children.* Los Angeles: Citadel Press.

Voice of the Child in Care (2004). *Start with the child, stay with the child.* London: NCB.

Wagner Report (1988). *Residential care: a positive choice* (Report of the independent review of residential care). London: HMSO.

Walton, R. & Elliott, D. (Eds.) (1980). *Residential care: a reader in current theory and practice.* Oxford: Pergamon Press.

Ward, A. (1993). *Working in group care.* Birmingham: BASW/Venture Press.

Ward, A. (1996). Opportunity led work: 2. The framework. *Social Work Education, 15*(3).

Ward, H., Skuse, T. & Munro, E.R. (2005). The best of times, the worst of times: young people's views of care and accommodation. *Adoption and Fostering, 29*(1), 8–17.

Weinstein, J., Whittington, C. & Leiba, T. (Eds.) (2003). *Collaboration in social work practice.* London: Jessica Kingsley Publishers.

West, M. (Ed.) (1996). *Handbook of work group psychology.* West Sussex: John Wiley and Sons.

Wheal, A. (2000). Speaking for themselves: two care leavers' experiences of residential care. In D. Crimmens and J. Pitts (Eds.), *Positive residential practice.* Lyme Regis: Russell House Publishing.

Whittington, C. & Bell, L. (2001). Learning from interprofessional and inter-agency practice in the new social work curriculum: evidence from an earlier research study. *Journal of Interprofessional Care, 15*(2), 153–169.

Whittington, C. (2003). Collaboration and partnership in context. In J. Weinstein, C. Whittington and T. Leiba (Eds.), *Collaboration in social work practice.* London: Jessica Kingsley Publishers.

Willumsen, E. & Hallberg, L. (2003). Interprofessional collaboration and young people in residential care: some professional perspectives. *Journal of Interprofessional Care, 17*(4), 389–400.

Wolfsenberger, W. (1972). *Normalisation: the principles of normalisation in human services.* Toronto: National Institute on Mental Retardation.

Inquiry reports

(The) Beckford Report (1985). *A child in trust: the report of the panel inquiry into the circumstances surrounding the death of Jasmine Beckford.* London Borough of Brent.

(The) Carlile Report (1987). *A child in mind: the protection of children in a responsible society: The report of the commission of inquiry into the circumstances surrounding the death of Kimberly Carlile.* London Borough of Greenwich.

(The) Cleveland Report (1988). *Report of the inquiry into child abuse in Cleveland 1987.* London: HMSO.

(The) Climbié Report (2003). *Report of an inquiry by Lord Laming.* London: HMSO.

(The) Clyde Report (1992). *Report of the inquiry into the removal of children from Orkney in February 1991.* Edinburgh: HMSO.

(The) Colwell Report (1974). *Report of the committee of inquiry into the care and supervision provided in relation to Maria Colwell.* London: HMSO.

(The) Curtis Report (1946). *The report of the care of children committee.* London: HMSO.

(The) Henry Report (1987). *Whose child? The report of the public inquiry into the death of Tyra Henry.* London Borough of Lambeth.

Levy, A. & Kahan, B. (1991). *The Pindown experience and the protection of children: The report of the Staffordshire Child Care Inquiry 1990.* Stafford: Staffordshire County Council.

(The) Ness Report (2003). *Report of the Caleb Ness inquiry.* Edinburgh: Lothian and Borders Child Protection Committee.

Index